Beyond Vegas

25 Exotic Wedding and Elopement Destinations Around the World

Lisa Tabb and Sam Silverstein

CB

CONTEMPORARY BOOKS

Library of Congress Cataloging-in-Publication Data

Tabb, Lisa.
　　Beyond Vegas : 25 exotic wedding and elopement destinations around the
world / Lisa Tabb and Sam Silverstein.
　　　　p.　　cm.
　　Includes index.
　　ISBN 0-8092-2883-1
　　1. Resorts—Guidebooks.　　2. Honeymoons.　　I. Silverstein, Sam.
II. Title.
TX907.T29　　2000
647.94—dc21

99-38573
CIP

Cover design by Todd Petersen
Cover and interior photographs courtesy of Lisa Tabb and Sam Silverstein
Interior design by Hespenheide Design

Published by Contemporary Books
A division of NTC/Contemporary Publishing Group, Inc.
4255 West Touhy Avenue, Lincolnwood (Chicago), Illinois 60712-1975 U.S.A.
Copyright © 2000 by Lisa Tabb and Sam Silverstein
Printed in the United States of America
International Standard Book Number: 0-8092-2883-1

00　01　02　03　04　05　ML　15　14　13　12　11　10　9　8　7　6　5　4　3　2　1

Contents

Acknowledgments

This book is dedicated to our parents, who raised us to follow our hearts wherever they may lead.

Working together to pull off an elopement turns strangers into intimates in a jiffy, and there are dozens of people whose magnitude in our memory belies the brevity of our encounter over the course of this project. Katrina Simorangkir, Putu Indrawati, Julia Gajcak, Denise Hewlett, Ivonne Torres, Martin Davidson, Kevin and Caron Tabb, Carl Spitzer and Karen Goldberg, Yuval Russ, Richard Evanson, Bob and Barbara Mandel, Suzanne Campioni-Tittoto, Sinjin Kelliher, Marcia Gordon, Bunny Shaw, Kuki Gallmann, Tove Gray-Stephens, Peter Llewellyn, Kurt Althof, Jay Pearson—we had the time of our lives thanks to your generosity.

Author Nelson DeMille introduced us to agent Nick Ellison who scored our deal with NTC/Contemporary Publishing. They all deserve our gratitude. Ditto Jill Davis, Kim Lisagor, Leigh Johnson, and Maria Lemus, who picked us up off the pavement short of the finish line and gave us the push we needed to complete the race. With this project, the accomplishment truly was in the journey.

Introduction

The original idea for *Beyond Vegas* was hatched during one of those years when it seemed that everyone in our immediate universe was planning a wedding. And no one appeared to be enjoying the experience. We were fielding phone call after phone call from exasperated friends and relatives, each of whom would unleash a long rant about the agony of developing their guest list or choosing a caterer or some such thing, then let out a sigh and say, "We should just elope." It occurred to us that a book of elopement options might enjoy a rabid audience . . . and provide an excuse for us to marry on the fly ourselves!

"Elope" is an elastic word, conjuring up a variety of scenarios. At one end of the spectrum you've got Las Vegas, which brings to mind images of fast-food wedding ceremonies attended by Elvis impersonators. A book that described how to elope in Las Vegas would be a short one, high on camp and low on scenery. This was not for us. We were interested in going *beyond* Vegas—literally and figuratively—and exploring the other end of the spectrum, places that are not only wedding friendly—with few or no residency requirements or bureaucratic hurdles involved in procuring a marriage license—but also tasteful and exotic.

So we started poking around. The word "elope" apparently gives wedding-industry types the willies. For some, the issue is business, or potential loss thereof. Two-inch-thick bridal magazines can't seem to find room for it. Publicity-hungry wedding planners flatly refused to deal with us when we explained to them the gist of our project.

For others, it's a matter of taste. Though the shelves of every bookstore in America are crammed with how-to guides to planning and executing conventional weddings, few of them so much as mention eloping. And those that do usually dress up the concept with sniffy references to "destination" or "far and away" weddings. None have had the guts to use the word "elope" on their cover.

Until now.

We eloped. In fact, we eloped ten times, obtaining marriage licenses, scheduling officiants, and repeating our vows again and again and again. We were married at a castle in Scotland and on a white sand beach in the British Virgin Islands, aboard a yacht in the Galápagos and beneath acacia trees in Kenya. In Jerusalem, our ceremony took place amid the ruins of a military citadel built two thousand years ago. In Fiji the bride arrived on a raft and then was carried ashore by men, Cleopatra-style, with nary a petal out of place in her bouquet. There was nothing tawdry or campy or careless about any of them (though we did save money; the conventional wedding industry's fears are real in that regard). We loved eloping. We had the time of our lives, ten times over. (A perfectly legal indulgence, by the way. U.S. law precludes marrying multiple partners but places no restrictions on the same couple marrying each other more than once.) This book is about our experiences—and how you can duplicate them if you wish—as well as a selection of additional elopement options we researched.

Know right at the top: *Beyond Vegas* is not intended to be used as a comprehensive travel guide to any of the destinations described within. A bonus for travelers is the degree to which eloping provides a glimpse into local people's daily lives wherever they happen to be. To spend a day at the attorney general's bare-bulb-lit office in Nairobi in search of a marriage license, for example, is to understand the source of Kenyans' great patience. But, for the volume of general information you should know before venturing abroad, you'll have to supplement what you see here with additional resources.

What *Beyond Vegas* is, is personal. Our firsthand experiences in each country are the basis of ten of the twenty-five chapters. In them are the stories of how we eloped: how we enlisted a squadron of Israeli army officers to hold our *huppah* in Jerusalem, how we happened to share a plate of fish and chips at a local coffee shop with the reverend who performed our ceremony in Scotland, how a family of warthogs delayed the start of our ceremony in Kenya. Our intention is to capture the spirit of what it is like to elope in each place, to provide a taste of what you might expect, to show through example what can be done. We're going for inspiration here as much as insight.

The other fifteen chapters we researched via the Internet, interviews with the principals, and so on. These chapters inevitably contain less descriptive detail than destinations we visited ourselves, but still aspire to provide a taste (if only a nibble) of the possibilities, as well as enough information to get started on the road toward visiting each place for yourselves. Let us know what you find out! It's our hope that subsequent editions of *Beyond Vegas* will add depth as well as breadth.

At the beginning of each chapter is a key intended to give a rough estimate of what each ceremony costs. It is highly subjective, but it's meant to represent our best guess at how much it costs to elope to each destination, not including travel expenses. (Who knows where you're coming from, after all?) One dollar sign is assigned to elopements in the neighborhood of $1,000 or less, two are for $2,000 or less, and so on up to four dollar signs, which indicates the most expensive options, $4,000 or more. Also included in each key is an indication of the amount of effort each undertaking will require. We've limited the difficulty scale to just three grades—everything described is either "no sweat," "moderate," or "doable"—to avoid scaring anyone off. Nothing we did, or heard about, would be described as "difficult" to pull off, certainly none more so than dealing with every detail of throwing a party for a hundred or more people right down to the shape of the folded napkins. If it's in *Beyond Vegas*, it's because it can be done.

Many chapters include sidebars on interesting activities, diversions, and local customs we encountered along the way. At the end of each chapter is a collection of nuts-and-bolts information on how to elope in each locale. We've tried to be as current as possible with regard to contact information, prices, and the like, but these are moving targets: be sure to double-check what you see here before packing your suitcase. And again, let us know of any corrections care of our publisher.

• • • • •

Eloping is not for everyone, and for couples who dream of walking down the aisle surrounded by friends and family (and bridesmaids and videographers and caterers), more power to you. We don't dare condemn it. But we had such a great time with this, it's hard for us not to proselytize.

Our top five reasons to elope:

1. **To save money.** Relatively speaking. Eloping is a bargain compared with the cost of conventional weddings, on which average couples spend in the neighborhood of $17,000 (according to *Modern Bride* magazine)—much more if they happen to live in a big city. With one exception, all of the elopements in this book, wedding and honeymoon included, cost less than $5,000 fully paid. It's our experience that you can stay at the best hotels, eat

like kings, see the world through a unique perspective, and return home marriage certificate in hand with enough dough left over to throw a whiz-bang reception if you wish.

2. To save time. Whereas a conventional wedding can consume a year or more of advance planning, our ceremonies were cobbled together in a matter of weeks—sometimes even days.

3. To preserve your sanity. Conventional weddings often are scripted down to the last flower petal; playing it loose is part of the thrill of eloping. Everything need not be perfect. When it's just the two of you, alone, with little to concentrate on besides one another, a slice of stale cake or a wrinkle in the bride's gown is far from the end of the world.

4. To have fun. You'll have to take our word on this one. Things have a way of coming together at the last minute when you elope. Hotel gardeners procure handfuls of flowers for the bride. Registrars agree to officiate on their days off. Passersby volunteer to take pictures or help translate instructions. Clouds part. Miracles happen. It's one of the joys of the whole adventure.

5. To be unusual. The elopement industry has just begun to blossom. Yet eloping is still a novelty in the sense that there are lots of choices out there and gobs of opportunities to differentiate yourselves from the herd. That's a good thing, no?

• • • • •

Many of these attributes also apply to destination weddings, which are essentially elopements plus guests. Given the luxury of time, the elopements depicted in *Beyond Vegas* are expandable to include family and friends.

The appendix contains lists, tables, and tidbits of advice that were left without a home elsewhere in the book. History suggests, however, that you'll have some questions that simply can't wait until the end for answers. There were several queries that seemed to keep popping up regardless of where in the world we happened to be during the year we spent on the road researching this book. Perhaps they have already occurred to you.

Does eloping abroad mean we're legally married?

Marriages that have been conducted legally abroad are recognized in the United States.

Is eloping hard to do?

Several of the elopements described would have been impossible to pull off without the aid of local wedding experts, especially where wrangling marriage licenses out of foreign city officials was concerned. But if you take anything away from this book, we hope it will be a sense of possibility. The subset of the world's nations with elopement-friendly waiting periods and marriage laws is still vast. Within them, if you can conjure a ceremony in your mind's eye, it's our experience someone out there can help pull it off.

And, of course . . .

How would we ever get divorced?

How rude of you to ask! Divorces generally are filed in the state in which a couple resides, regardless of where the wedding itself took place. If you must know.

Part I

Europe

In all of Europe, only a handful of countries' residency requirements are elopement-friendly. You can go ahead and cross that dream Devonshire country estate off your list of quickie wedding destinations—couples wishing to be married in England must arrive a minimum of eighteen days in advance.

Ditto that Côte d'Azur chateau whose picture you've had pinned to your wall. France's nonresident waiting period is thirty days. C'est la vie.

What's left is hardly the dregs, however. Scotland, Italy, Greece, and Switzerland contain sufficient romantic nooks and crannies to entertain armies of elopers. We've highlighted one elopement scenario in each country, three of which we experienced firsthand.

Scotland

Cost: $

Degree of difficulty: No sweat

Our ceremony at the Stonefield Castle Hotel on the shores of Loch Fyne west of Glasgow began with a chat in the lobby. Reverend Montgomery, an octogenarian retiree from the nearby town of

The Stonefield Castle Hotel on the shores of Loch Fyne, Argyll, Scotland

Tayvallich, is the hotel manager's first phone call when guests turn up seeking to tie the knot. He had agreed to officiate our ceremony on short notice—we arrived on Wednesday and were wed that Friday—so long as we'd take the time to sit with him beforehand while he enjoyed a *rollie* (a handmade cigarette stuffed with pipe tobacco) and some conversation. Eloping in Scotland is an informal affair through and through.

In fact, for centuries all that was required of two people who wished to be married in Scotland was that they declare their bond publicly: no vows, rings, or clergy necessary. Reverend Montgomery's eyes flashed mischievously at the very thought of it. Scottish weddings now typically take place in churches. "But it's not traditional!" he said, flipping his hands at right angles for emphasis. The conversation wended its way through a variety of topics ranging from "the troubles" in Northern Ireland to favorite local fishing holes. Reverend Montgomery's resonant voice and the morning sun streaming through the curtains made us feel sleepy, despite the adrenaline produced by wearing wedding attire in public. A relaxed feeling on your wedding day is a rare enough treat. This was downright cozy.

The Stonefield Castle Hotel has been the site of dozens of wedding ceremonies over the years, from blowouts to intimate little affairs such as our own. The general manager, Peter Llewellyn, an eminently agreeable lad, is available to help with logistics ranging from floral arrangements to a festive *ceilidh* (pronounced "kady") band complete with dance lessons. For a crowning touch, it's hard to beat haggis for dinner, marched into the dining room to the tune of a bleating bagpipe. The local piper hired for such occasions has a flair for the dramatic, and has been known to recite several stanzas of Robert Burns before pulling a dagger from his sock and administering the ceremonial first cut.

Eilean Donan Castle, among the most photographed locales in all of Scotland (Courtesy of Highland Dreams)

Peter offered to arrange for a local florist to provide us with a bouquet for Lisa and a boutonniere for Sam, but the grounds of the hotel itself happened to be bursting with flowering hydrangea at the time of our visit. With the general manager's permission, while Reverend Montgomery changed from his dark suit into a ceremonial smock, we wandered the lawn with a pair of scissors in search of the perfect half-dozen stems. Our stroll was illuminated by the first sustained rays of sun we'd experienced since our arrival in the British Isles seventy-two hours before. During a round of golf the previous day in Campbeltown, we had seen proscribed patches of sunlight dancing on the Atlantic but also raindrops the size of clams. We picked a bouquet of powder-blue hydrangea, which happened to set off Lisa's cream-colored dress, and enjoyed the warmth of the sun on the backs of our necks.

Given the choice of facing either the hotel or Loch Fyne for our ceremony, we chose the castle. That this particular stone citadel never actually repelled marauding Jacobites detracted from its drama not at all. Its towers protruded steeply against the blue sky above the landing on which we stood, and the dark streaks of moisture on the stone walls evaporated in misty wisps. Reverend Montgomery's aged countenance and leathery voice fit the mood to a tee.

Peter handled the snapshots. For the first part of our ceremony, Reverend Montgomery read from a script. The words were pleasantly godly, but not overly so. Then he invited us to speak some vows to each other and to exchange rings. Sun streamed through the clouds in torrents and reflected brightly off the loch, lending the hotel's sandstone bricks a peach-colored hue. As the barometric pressure rose, the sound of the wind in a stand of nearby pines required Reverend Montgomery to add a little oomph to his rich voice as he pronounced us husband and wife.

We picked the bridal bouquet of hydrangeas from a garden on the grounds of our hotel.

• • • • •

Castle Riding Centre

Horseback riding is an ideal mode for exploring Scotland. The pace is leisurely but still efficient. It feels historical. And best of all, it is more social than driving around surrounded by steel. Conversation with the effusive locals is one of the joys of visiting Scotland.

In Argyll, Tove Gray-Stephens's Castle Riding Centre dominates the local equestrian scene. Gray-Stephens, from Norway, was the first woman to ski the highest peak in her native country, was a formidable rally driver in her day, and once worked as a stunt rider for feature films (*The Master of Ballantrae*). Today she operates a championship stable on the grounds of her late husband's centuries-old farmhouse in Ardrishaig. Guided trips lasting up to a week or more, centering around themes such as gourmet food or following in Rob Roy's hoofprints, are for advanced equestrians. Dilettantes such as ourselves are happy just to spend the day exploring her farm.

During our visit, Lisa was assigned to Fröya, the filly Tove rode on film. Elegant did not begin to describe her. "You're riding a film star," said our guide, Sheryl, walking Fröya around to a small landing to make it easier for Lisa to climb into her saddle for the first time. Once both of us were aboard our respective mounts, Sheryl demonstrated how to hold the reins British style ("like ice cream cones") and off we went.

The first minutes of our ride wended above the farmhouse, through a pasture. Skittish young sheep ducked between their mothers' legs as we ambled past. Highland cattle were bolder; they gathered by the side of the trail to watch the parade, their view obscured by unruly locks of hair that fell comically in front of their almost-human eyes.

When the sun hits Argyll, it sparkles. Loch Fyne, the damp pasture, even the freshly shorn sheep, all took on an intensity of color that made our heads, already woozy from the low barometric pressure of the region, spin. The horses walked happily, stopping at our command so that we could snap photos or of their own volition to munch on thistles and grass. Water that pooled in trailside streams was the color of whiskey; Sheryl chatted good-

A day on horseback at the Castle Riding Centre presents lots of photo ops.

naturedly about the correct pronunciation of local single malts ("It's la-fraig, not la-frog!"), as well as about the series of life decisions that had led her to ride horses in the countryside for a living. Eventually we strung out along the trail and sauntered along in silence, blissfully happy just to absorb the view.

The Castle Riding Centre also hosts weddings on horseback, officiated by a local minister who happens to be a crack equestrian. Ceremonies are followed by a reception dinner at the Stonefield Castle Hotel.

For more information, contact the Castle Riding Centre directly by phone at 011-44-1546-603274, or E-mail castleridingcentre@brenfield.demon.co.uk. You can also call Cross Country International Equestrian Vacations at 800-828-8768.

Our hard-earned appetites were indulged with gusto at the Stonefield Castle Hotel each night. More a country home than a castle per se—Stonefield's original occupants, the Campbells, built the estate in 1837, which is yesterday by Scottish standards—the facility still has a pleasantly aged air. Old, big, damp, appointed with velvet-draped furniture and broad spiral staircases, the building retains much of its original atmosphere, despite extensive renovations in the fifty years it's been operated as a hotel. Enormous portraits of Mrs. Campbell and her rosy-cheeked children still hang in the hallway at the base of the main stairs.

The heart of the place is its restaurant. Surrounded on three sides by glass, the elegant room (jackets required) features a fine view of Loch Fyne, the source of most items on the menu. A typical

The kiss: Scotland

night's offerings included trout, gravlax, salmon fillets in pastry, venison, sea bass, duck, heaping plates of buttered veggies served on the side, and creamy butterscotch pudding. If you time it right, toward the end of each evening's sitting, the cheerful staff offer second helpings of dessert. Scotland is not necessarily known for its cuisine (subsequent forays into the local village's restaurants confirmed why), but at Stonefield Castle Hotel we ate like kings.

Our appetites were supplemented by the raw weather. The view from the glass-walled restaurant changed from meal to meal, depending on the intensity of the cloud cover. Some evenings, Loch Fyne was obscured entirely, even while the tide lapped against the foundation of the room. On those nights, the restaurant's sense of intimacy was amplified by the surrounding gloom, and we sat—huddled really—together at the same corner of our table.

After dinner, it is traditional to retire to a paneled bar adjacent to the restaurant for a wee dram of whiskey. There also are two sitting rooms at the hotel, still decorated with the Campbells' original furnishings: marble fireplaces, velvet couches and high-backed chairs, weighty mirrors, and impenetrable drapes with tassels. The ornate environs are ideal for whiling away stormy nights with a drink and a book.

On our wedding day, we chose to bypass the hotel restaurant and opted instead to visit a local fish-and-chips shop for lunch, in

Presenting . . .

the name of experience. By coincidence, seated in a booth by the window were Reverend Montgomery and his wife. They beckoned us to sit with them at their tiny booth. Everything in Scotland is cozy.

• • • • •

Stonefield Castle Hotel rooms fall into two categories: those with views of the loch, and those with views of the parking lot. Try for the former, but you won't be mortified with the latter. Rooms range from $80 to $120 during the summer (already a bargain), yet are discounted as much as 30 percent during the off-season. Dinner and breakfast are included.

For weddings, Stonefield Castle staff will happily arrange for a bagpiper (approximately $125), wedding cake ($250), and other accoutrements with prior notice. For more information, call 011-44-1880-820836 or visit www.celticcastles.com/castles/stonefield.

Elsewhere in Scotland

Before we go any further, *do not* elope in Scotland if heavy weather is not your thing. Not only does it rain a lot here, it does so with gusto.

That said, if you're the sort of person who enjoys the occasional storm or two—as well as verdant countryside, centuries-old castles, and heroically friendly locals—Scotland is guaranteed to pluck your heartstrings. Here are some options.

Gleneagles

Gleneagles is a luxurious resort set on an 830-acre estate in Perthshire, north of and halfway between Edinburgh and Glasgow, that revolves around three championship golf courses and a golf academy. Though they don't do on-course weddings as such, it's not impossible to be wed there in the morning and then play your first round as a legitimate twosome that afternoon. Shooting, fishing, a day spa, and a top-shelf equestrian center also vie for guests' attention. For more information, phone Gleneagles directly at 011-44-1764-662231.

Gretna Green

Although Scotland and England technically have been part of the same United Kingdom since the early eighteenth century, England has always had more stringent marriage laws. Hence Gretna Green, a picturesque village just inside the Scottish border that has been a popular "runaway wedding" stop for a couple of centuries and counting.

Among several facilities in Gretna Green that still are maintained with weddings in mind, the Old Blacksmith's Shop is perhaps the most historic. The shop, located at the confluence of five thoroughfares, is where couples once were wed fresh off the stagecoach. Legal ceremonies are still performed here. For more information, call 011-44-1461-338441.

The Gretna Marriage Registration Office mails out information packages that contain information on hotels, photographers, and other local wedding services, as well as the necessary legal papers. To get yours, call 011-44-1461-337648.

Castles

Duns Castle, in southern Scotland ten miles inland from the North Sea, is a secluded property enveloped by woodlands and a lake. A single family has owned the property since 1696, and now operates a bed-and-breakfast out of the castle that's ideal for weddings.

Dundas, eight miles outside Edinburgh, is one of the most beautiful castles in all of Scotland. The original structure dates back to the fourteenth century. A more modern facility, built in 1818 by the great Scottish architect William Burn, stands on the site today. For more information on both Dundas and Duns, contact Scottish Wedding Consultants at 011-44-1875-320490, or see www.scottishweddingconsultants.co.uk.

Eilean Donan Castle, perched on an islet on Loch Duich on Scotland's west coast, is perhaps the most photographed monument in all the land. Visitors approach the three-story structure via a narrow footbridge. A clear day offers views of the Isle of Skye and the chance to snap the castle's reflection in the loch. For more information, contact Highland Belles Weddings at 011-44-1349-867665.

Rua Reidh

The Rua Reidh Lighthouse, situated on a peninsula in the hardscrabble northwest Highlands, three miles from its nearest neighbor, has to be one of the more remote places on the entire planet

Golf in the Kingdom

Though Argyll is not on a par with St. Andrews, the cradle of the game, there is golf to be played. And it *is* Scotland. For hacks such as ourselves, that's enough. Our first outing was at the local course in Inveraray, one of three nine-hole tracks within easy striking distance of our hotel.

Elsewhere in the world, and even elsewhere in Scotland, golf can be a priggish pastime. But at its roots the game is an egalitarian one, a tradition that lives on at the Inveraray Golf Club. Here the local council has chosen to spend its available funds on facilities other than the clubhouse, which consists of four exposed lattices of drywall, a roof, and a door. Nailed to the shed's outside wall is a drop box in which visitors are invited to deposit their greens fees honor-system style. Our company on the first tee—the only other people on the course, apparently— were a husband and wife from nearby Tarbert, out for a brisk round before dinner. We let them go ahead for fear of embarrassing ourselves and our country.

The course itself is hilly and long, with little evidence of its exotic (to us) locale except for the stirring view of Inveraray Castle from the fourth fairway. On the sixth, we encountered two neighborhood boys swimming in a water hazard. When Sam's approach landed in the drink, they happily retrieved his ball.

Our golf legs now established, the next day we made the pilgrimage to Machrihanish, an hour-plus south along the A83 near Campbeltown. Machrihanish is a Scottish-style links course straight from central casting, replete with a howling wind off the Atlantic and acres of uncut gorse lining each fairway (and often blanketing the first hundred yards between tee and landing area). Machrihanish ate golf balls like popcorn. We tore up our scorecards on the front nine and soaked in the scenery.

to get hitched. For a total immersion experience, stay at the keeper's quarters, which have been converted into a guest house. For more information, contact Highland Belles Weddings at 011-44-1349-867665.

Nuts and Bolts

Where to Start

Scotland's marriage laws are perhaps the most accommodating in all of Europe, and getting married here without the aid of a local wedding coordinator is easy. The locals' English skills are a considerable help in this regard.

The first step is to determine the location of your ceremony, then deal directly with the registrar for that region. The nearest registry to the Stonefield Castle Hotel is in Inveraray. Contact Mrs. E. Bell (telephone and fax 011-44-1546-886388) for more information. The main marriage registry in Edinburgh will help you locate local registrars elsewhere in Scotland. Call 011-44-131-3144447 or see www.open.gov.uk/gros/faq.htm#marriage.

The end of the Isle: Rua Reidh Lighthouse, in the northwest Highlands
(Courtesy of Highland Dreams)

Travel Information

British Airways offers direct nonstop flights from the United States (New York) to Glasgow, but we laid over in London for a night, just for kicks. For more information, contact British Airways at 800-247-9297.

Legal Requirements

You will need to submit the following documents (via fax, if you wish) fifteen days in advance to the registrar nearest where your ceremony will take place: a marriage notice (application), copies of your birth certificates, and a certificate of nonimpediment to marriage from your local registrar in the States.

For civil ceremonies performed at a registry office, the marriage schedule (license) and all applicable fees add up to £114 (approximately U.S.$187). Religious ceremonies conducted by ministers are approximately one third the cost, until you take the tip into account. Reverend Montgomery worked for a hand-shake—we chipped in £60 (the equivalent of U.S.$100) on our own accord.

Lead Time

As stated earlier, the paperwork needs to be filed (via fax) with the registrar a minimum fifteen days in advance, but divorced or widowed applicants should triple their lead time. Though there is no official residency requirement, if your ceremony will be offici-ated by a minister you will need to visit the registrar's office in per-son to pick up your schedule (license). In theory, this could happen the same day as your ceremony. But registrars' hours vary wildly, and it's a good idea to give yourselves some wiggle room.

Note that, following your ceremony, you also need to deliver the signed schedule to the registrar within three days.

When to Go

The weather in Scotland is predictably stormy September through April, and unpredictably so the rest of the year. From May through early June, the grounds of the Stonefield Castle Hotel are awash in Himalayan rhododendrons in full bloom. A yachting series on the loch each May adds to the hotel's festive air, especially the bar.

Additional Contact Information

An excellent source for information about the Argyll region, and all of Scotland for that matter, is www.argyllonline.co.uk. The British Tourist Authority phone number is 800-462-2748.

Take Our Advice

The journey from Glasgow to the Stonefield Castle Hotel is three hours of pure stress if you're used to driving on the right side of the road. Book your rental car as early as possible so you can reserve one with an automatic transmission (extremely scarce in these parts). It's more expensive, but you won't have to worry about remembering to shift in a backward H with your left hand.

Our favorite whiskey is Oban: sweet, strong, restorative. The locals drink everything neat, but no one will break a chair over your head if you order your dram on the rocks.

The only possible pitfall to a Scottish elopement is the weather. But even this dark cloud has its silver lining: romantic is a nice, flexible adjective that certainly includes stormy days spent indoors beside a crackling fire, sipping whiskey and leafing through dusty volumes of vivid poetry.

Recommended Reading

Take along anything by Robert Burns, Scotland's beloved balladeer and national poet.

Italy

Cost: $$$$

Degree of difficulty: Doable

If you ask for a slice of pizza at the train station in Padua, you're going to get a deliciously grainy round of Italian flat bread topped with Italian red sauce and Italian mozzarella, perhaps a bottle of Italian water on the side. You cannot go wrong in this country, whether you're dining at a four-star hotel or at a rest stop. Italy is all about standards.

Inside the station, the departure board was full of towns with names that were familiar to us from wine labels and high school Shakespeare: Verona, Venice, Chianti, and so on. We were headed through Castelfranco to the village of Asolo, in the Veneto region of northeast Italy—a verdant slice of gentle countryside dotted with vineyards and great villas (mansions) built by wealthy nobles of the Venetian Republic during its sixteenth-, seventeenth-, and eighteenth-century heyday. Our train ride took us back in time; the last rays of the day illuminated Padua's unimpressive suburbs, then corn fields, and then a glimpse of a castle. We continued to peer hopefully out the window even after it had gone dark.

Asolo is home base for Campioni Italiani di Veneto, a decoratively named and logoed tour company that essentially boils down to one person: Suzanne Campion-Tittoto. The company is rooted in romance. Born in New York City of Italian-American

In Venice romance is a given, and walking is not an option.

(Courtesy of Ente Nazionale Italiano Per Il Turismo)

parents, Campion-Tittoto was visiting relatives in Asolo several years ago when she ran into a childhood friend she had not seen for twenty-two years. He told her that he had been in love with her all that time. They were married soon after.

Suzanne is the authority in all things di Veneto, fluent in Italian, a gracious host, and an ace wedding coordinator—a total whirlwind. Our directions to her had been: "We want to get married, and we want to ride bikes around the countryside." From that scant guidance Suzanne created an itinerary that consumed three full days.

First on the list was a legitimate meal. Suzanne checked us into our hotel, Albergo Al Sole, and pointed us toward a café within walking distance that had agreed to stay open late for us. Asolo at night seemed purposefully lit to accentuate its architectural drama. The heart of the city is an open space, Piazza Garibaldi, surrounded on all sides by porticoed structures with darkened shops on their ground floors. Shadowy elements towering overhead promised to make an even grander impression in daylight.

A carafe of local red wine arrived with the first course, a caprese salad. Who knows why Italian mozzarella and tomatoes are better than our mozzarella and tomatoes? But they are. Then twin plates of pasta, one with tuna, one plain, appeared. Who knows why their pasta—merely eggs, flour, and water—is better than our pasta? But it is.

• • • • •

Breakfast the following morning on a balcony adjoining Albergo Al Sole's dining room provided a bird's-eye view of the town itself, elevated several hundred feet above the Veneto Plain. (At the apex of the hill on which Asolo is built stands a medieval fortress, La Rocca, that serves as a reference point for miles in every direction.) Every building in our immediate vicinity—the cathedral, Queen Caterina Cornaro's castle, the shops—was a variation on the same architectural themes and materials: arches and porticos, stone and wrought iron, orange terra cotta and layered tile. Asolo's walls are attractively aged in the way every

Old meets new at Albergo Al Sole. Our room featured a modern spa shower and hand-milled soap made from local lavender.

trendy restaurant built in the United States in the last decade has sandpapered itself silly trying to emulate.

Suzanne met us after breakfast to get us launched on our bike tour. She provided maps and directions while the hotel supplied a pair of road/mountain bike hybrids in good repair. We were directed to take the road toward Cornudo, past Villa Dimarco, toward the foothills of the Dolomites (where we could stop for some prime hang-gliding, if we wished).

A leisurely ride and lunch were more our speed. To this end, we parked our bikes at a gourmet shop within one hundred yards of our hotel and loaded up on the raw materials for a killer picnic: sun-dried tomatoes, local cheese, artichoke hearts, porcini mushrooms in oil, bread, some arugula for greenery, and a bottle of San Peligrino. Our plan was to pick up the wine at a shop or winery

Ennio's

If you ever find yourself in Asolo, go out of your way to visit Ennio's Gourmet Shop on Via R. Browning across from the fountain. The shop is packed to its ancient rafters with treasures: pasta in a rainbow of colors and jumble of shapes, mysterious Italian candies by the barrelful, acres of local cheese in a cooler by the register. An entire annex room is set aside for Ennio's selection of *grappa* (wine) in bottles designed to be admired like jewels. During our visit, the sun angled through the portico outside the shop and into the room, which glittered like the palace of Oz.

along our route. This proved to be harder than we'd imagined, however. The first leg of our ride was pleasantly downhill, past farmhouses and outcroppings of roadside lavender. The second leg was all uphill—we'd taken the wrong road out of town and had to start over. By the time we finally were pointed in the right direction, it was midday and the shops in the surrounding countryside were shuttered so that their proprietors could enjoy an afternoon nap.

The road toward Cornudo is a scenic one, though the frequency of dairy trucks required that we pay as much attention to our girth as to the view. There were vineyards, many of which grow a local grape, *prosecco*, which produces a sweetish wine that's delicious either *tranquillo* (still) or *frizzante*. And there were villas, opulent and enormous, yet designed in concert with the landscape in a way that was the opposite of ostentatious. Italians even know how to show off gracefully. Sprinkled here and there along the roadside were glimpses of the twentieth century. The Veneto also is popular among major manufacturers, including Bennetton and Nordica. Resisting the siren song of primo outlet shopping required an act of will.

The Veneto region is known for its ornate villas.

At the fringe of a particularly dense expanse of vineyards we encountered a handlettered sign on a lone pole: vino. We whipped our bikes hard left and bumped along a dirt track for a quarter mile or so before encountering the source, a nondescript farm. In the yard of the farmhouse an aged woman in a flowered dress was emptying a plate of melon rinds into her compost pile. In pidgin Italian—the locals are thankfully tolerant in this regard—we asked if there were wine for sale on the premises.

"Prosecco," was her reply.

"Si, processed," Lisa said.

Recognizing our confusion, the woman marched us decisively past a brutish-looking guard dog toward the barn, unfastened a padlock, and leaned against a heavy door. Inside were two fermentation tanks and a small tower of pallets stacked with green bottles that were capped with crimped tin. Pay dirt. Glasses materialized, and generous samples were poured from a polished brass tank. The wine was tingly with ongoing fermentation and fantastically light—a delicious match for a sweaty bike ride on a humid day. When our sipping devolved into conversation before our glasses were entirely empty, the proprietor pantomimed offense and insisted we drink every last drop.

Through hand gestures and frantic forays into our Berlitz guide it was determined that we were not students, this was our honeymoon (we didn't get into the details), and we were staying in Asolo. We lived in San Francisco. We enjoyed her wine very much. For L5,000 (U.S.$3) she agreed to part with a full bottle and bid us a hearty *arrivedirci*. A pat for the dog and we were back on our bikes, high as kites.

A quieter, though steeper, side road took us back toward Asolo. In spots where shade or lush roadside vegetation provided a hint of cool, we dismounted to gawk at the impressive villas. Despite our languid pace, the road returned us to Asolo before we'd found a suitable spot for our picnic, so we enjoyed our second meal of the day on the scenic balcony of our hotel, assembling our sandwiches on borrowed china while the town below us slept off the afternoon heat.

Immediately outside Albergo Al Sole's front entrance is a cobblestone parking lot worn slippery by years of use. In the lobby is a modern art installation which rotates daily. The dichotomy is a metaphor for all of Asolo, which literally offers the best of both worlds, old and new. Rooms start at $350 per night. You can work through Campioni Italiani di Veneto to book a room, or contact Albergo Al Sole directly at 011-39-423-528111.

Typical of the Veneto, Asolo City Hall is housed in a centuries-old villa.

• • • • •

It would be nice to be able to say that our wedding day dawned to pealing bells from the cathedral, but in fact we'd been up for an hour, shopping for the appropriate bottle of *grappa* to present to the mayor as a token of gratitude for officiating our ceremony, when we heard the daily chime. Buying Italian spirits for an Italian is intimidating to say the least. After several long minutes of indecision, we went with the most festively pretty bottle we could find, wholly ignorant of its contents.

At 11 A.M., Suzanne met us at our hotel and escorted us the hundred yards or so to Asolo City Hall. Here we hooked up with our photographer, Piero Ferrajolo, and a city official who escorted us to a huge, wood-floored chamber outside the mayor's closed doors. Asolo City Hall is housed in a villa that dates back about five centuries. Portraits of the founding family, the Beltraminis, still hang on the walls, and their accumulated treasures—including ornaments from the Orient—decorate the building.

The mayor, wearing a ceremonial red sash over his Oxford shirt, emerged from his office and shook hands all around, then gestured for us to arrange ourselves around a microphone-festooned table in the chamber normally used for city council meetings. A smattering of city employees gathered on a balcony overhead as word spread of our presence.

The ceremony began with the mayor reading from our wedding contract a passage stating the "bonds of marriage" and the legal responsibilities of each spouse. Suzanne translated discreetly,

The mayor was a good sport.

one paragraph at a time. Then vows, then the rings, then a kiss. Applause from the civil servants who were gathered on the balcony echoed in the enormous room (a ballroom!).

The ceremony concluded with us adding our signatures to a huge book, in which were recorded the names of all couples married on the spot dating back a hundred years or more. Though Italian ceremonies may be held virtually anywhere, the contract and book signing must be done in a city hall or Roman Catholic church. The deed now officially done, the mayor invited us to see his office. Inside, more of the Beltraminis' treasures were on display. In one corner, snapshots of the mayor's family stood on an ornately carved, three-hundred-year-old chest of drawers.

Our photographer—whose father and grandfather had also been Asolo's portraitists— marched us down seemingly every street in the city.

Our photographer, Piero—whose father and grandfather also had been Asolo's portraitists—snapped furiously while waving us through a variety of poses in the mayor's office. Italian couples traditionally create an album of their wedding day that's as elaborate (and costly) as any element of the ceremony. We tried to opt for a simpler tack, but Piero was not easily dissuaded. Once we'd presented our bottle of *grappa* to the mayor, Piero chronicled our exit from city hall step by step. He then marched us down seemingly every street in the city in search of backdrops to shoot us against.

Still in our finery, we proceeded to the Hotel Villa Cipriani on Via Canova for a celebratory lunch. This Asolo establishment is an offshoot of the renowned four-star Venice hotel at which Ernest Hemingway used to frequent Harry's Bar (and where Giuseppe Cipriani poured the first prosecco and peach juice Bellini).

The dining room had a luminous glow one doesn't normally associate with midday meals—an effect only accentuated by the Bellinis, an impending rain storm, and the residual adrenaline of our ceremony. After an appetizer of battered zucchini flowers, a bottle of expertly matched white wine arrived with our primi course of lobster salad. Then flat noodles with scampi, risotto with mushrooms, and fruit salad for dessert. The storm moved over the hotel midway through our meal and washed against the dining room's windows, blurring our view of a comically tall and skinny villa, Contarini Mocenigo, on an adjacent hillside. The clincher: the best cappuccino we've ever tasted. In seventy-two hours in Italy we had no less than four spectacular meals, ranging from the caprese salad at the local café the night of our arrival to the lavish wedding luncheon. You simply can't go wrong in this country.

Elsewhere In Italy...

Suzanne Campion-Tittoto provided us with all of the following suggestions.

Florence

Wed in the cradle of the Italian Renaissance, home of Dante, Machiavelli, Michelangelo, and the Medicis. Florence's charm is rooted in its location on the banks of the Arno River, surrounded

Florence and the Arno River
(Courtesy of Ente Nazionale Italiano Per Il Turismo)

by verdant countryside. The Palazzo Vecchio, built by Arnolfo di Cambio between 1299 and 1314, is an ideal spot for civil ceremonies. Other options in villas abound.

Cortona

Ah, Tuscany. Set on a hillside among ancient olive groves, the town of Cortona is little changed since the Middle Ages. Couples have a choice of wedding locations: the town hall, which was built in the sixteenth century and features historic Renaissance frescoes, or the chapel of an exquisite villa, which once served as the home of poet Antonio Guadagnoli. Either way, the surrounding olive- and vineyard-blanketed Tuscan countryside is at your door.

Ah, Tuscany
(Courtesy of Ente Nazionale Italiano Per Il Turismo)

Perugia

Here couples are wed in a castle on a hill, with surrounding views of the Umbrian countryside. The castle is straight from a movie; squint a bit and you may be able to see rival noblemen crossing their foils in the rosebush-strewn garden.

Sorrento and the Amalfi Coast

At a villa by the sea, the atmosphere is pungent with the aroma of flowers and salt air. The romantic island of Capri is within easy traveling distance, an ideal wedding-honeymoon combo.

In Sorrento, on the Amalfi Coast, the atmosphere is scented by the sea.
(Courtesy of Ente Nazionale Italiano Per Il Turismo)

Venice

Get married in the most romantic city in the world, in a palace that dates all the way back to the Venetian Republic. Transportation to and from the ceremony is via gondola, of course.

Verona

In Fair Verona we lay our scene at a pair of castles that, according to legend, belonged to the rival Montagues and Capulets. As in Romeo Montague and Juliet Capulet. What more romantic place could there be for a wedding?

Agriturismo

Much of the Veneto region's charm lies in its agrarian character. The disfiguring effects of industrialization have largely missed this swath of vineyards and lush forest, which is as appealing today as it was when the wealthiest nobles in Venice were enticed to build their country villas here centuries ago.

Farmland is as difficult to preserve in northern Italy as anywhere else, however, and to help stem the tide of development many landowners have opened their doors to outsiders. Lodging ranges from luxury accommodations in renovated farmhouses to rented rooms in the homes of actual farm workers. To qualify as an *agriturismo* or a farm-based bed-and-breakfast (and thus receive a government subsidy), meals must consist of ingredients grown on the premises. Agriturismo meals typically are straightforward but primally satisfying parades of pasta, fresh bread, vegetables, meat, cheese, and local wine—at a considerable savings over a conventional restaurant. Don't miss this unique experience.

Nuts and Bolts

Where to Start

Italy is old, scenic, and bountiful—anywhere you go is going to be great. Eloping here, however, is kind of a grind. There's lots of paperwork involved, and few Italian wedding professionals are willing to help couples who wish to get married quickly. Couples planning elaborate ceremonies, with the luxury of long lead times, will be met with greater enthusiasm.

Suzanne Campion-Tittoto is the exception to this rule. In addition to an impeccable grasp of Italian laws, customs, and culture—particularly with regard to Venice and the Veneto—her preternatural can-do spirit is perfectly suited for eloping. If Suzanne can't arrange something, it can't be done. Call Campioni Italiani di Veneto's Los Angeles office at 888-4-VENETO (888-483-6386) or 310-373-2226 and see for yourself.

Travel Information

Alitalia is foremost among a number of major carriers that fly non-stop from the United States to Milan, with connections to the airport in Venice. For more information, call 800-223-5730.

From Venice it's an hour drive on to Asolo. The nearest train station is Castelfranco, twenty minutes from Asolo by taxi.

Legal Requirements

Procuring a marriage license in Italy is not easily done and should only be attempted with the help of a professional. Know that the process requires a thirty-day head start (for simple civil ceremonies), birth certificates with apostile stamps (authorization from the secretary of state from where you were born), passports, and a statement by two witnesses that you are free to marry—all translated into Italian.

The paperwork associated with procuring a marriage license in Italy can cost $400 or more. Campioni Italiani di Veneto passes these fees along at cost as part of their wedding-honeymoon combination packages, which run well into four figures.

Lead Time

Campioni Italiani di Veneto requires at least thirty days' prior notice to arrange weddings. However, couples need not arrive in Italy more than two days in advance of their ceremony.

When to Go

The best time to visit the Veneto and beat the heat, cold, and crowds are the shoulder seasons, April through June and September through October.

Additional Contact Information

There are three Italian State Tourist Offices in the United States: New York (212-245-4822), Los Angeles (310-820-2977), and Chicago (312-644-0990).

One Thing We Wish We'd Known Beforehand

The Veneto is prime biking country, gently contoured and dense with distractions. If we'd scheduled sufficient time, Suzanne would have created an itinerary that covered more ground (via quieter roads). There's no reason to rush anything in Italy.

Recommended Reading

Victorian poet Robert Browning lived in Asolo for three separate intervals and named his last volume of poetry *Asolando* in its honor.

Greece

Cost: $$

Degree of difficulty: No sweat

The Greek island of Mykonos is perhaps the most accommodating place on the planet to muddle through a crippling case of jet lag. Napping away the heat of the day—rousing only to nibble bricks of salted white cheese or sip a cold Olympic beer—is perfectly acceptable here, encouraged even. Everyone else on the island will be sleeping off the previous evening's disco session anyway.

If your addled internal clock finds you awake at odd hours, that's fine too. Insomniacs are rewarded early each morning with the most placid hours of the day, before the island's narrow streets begin to clog with mopeds and taxis headed for some power shopping in Mykonos's capital, Mykonos Town (Hora), or radiating out toward the island's myriad beaches. During our visit, even after our sleep routines had returned to some semblance of normal, we continued to make a point of rising at sunrise each morning to enjoy quiet breakfasts in the gentlest light and bracing dips in the Aegean Sea.

Our home for the week was an apartment at Costa Ilios, a cluster of whitewashed buildings located on a spit of rock that juts into the Aegean approximately two miles south of Mykonos Town. The morning of our arrival, the sound of our rapping on the "reception" door at 8 A.M. echoed throughout the apartment complex. We had yet to learn that no one on Mykonos is voluntarily awake at that hour, never mind at work behind a desk. Eventually, we abandoned our bags and backtracked a mile or so along the access road toward a supermarket we'd spied from our taxi. Our initiative was borne of necessity: once the adrenaline of our arrival wore off, we were due for a major crash. If we didn't stock up on some staples ASAP, it might be days before we again escaped our apartment.

The Cyclades—so named because of the way they encircle the island of Delos, once the capital of all classical Greece—comprise about two dozen inhabitable landmasses rooted sturdily in the windswept Aegean. Each island's personality is distinct, and impact from tourism varies widely. All, however, share an affinity for white cubist architecture (the adjective "cycladic" describes this style the world over), and all are arid and rocky to a degree that borders on lunar. Our airborne approach had provided a startling survey of Mykonos's virtually treeless surface. Upon closer inspection during our walk, we found rocks indeed predominate. Boundaries between neighbors are marked by crude stone walls, which soak up enough excess basalt to create small patches of grass for goats and the occasional horse to graze.

Against this stark landscape, the white homes stand out like dollops of whipped cream, and the Aegean's already otherworldly blue is amplified to near incandescence. Bordering the colorless land, the water here appears computer-enhanced, like a vivid product in an otherwise black-and-white advertisement.

At the supermarket, we picked our way through rows of brightly packaged supplies until we arrived at a glass display case that held the good stuff: local *kopanisti* goat cheese, plump Kalamata olives, yogurt. Ah, the yogurt! A young woman behind the case spooned ladlefuls into a tub for us; it was the consistency of honey and pure white.

When we returned to Costa Ilios, we scarfed down our first helping of yogurt, then marched immediately upstairs to bed. Our sleeping room featured a ceiling fan and a single window that opened onto the Aegean. It was prime. Thus concluded the first day of our elopement in the Cyclades.

Any night of the week Mykonos Town is alive with chattery bars and pulsating discos, patronized by impeccably tanned divas in towering heels and young men of myriad nationalities in nearly identical white linen shirts. If your concept of eloping includes a little nightlife, stay as close to downtown as you can stand.

We prefer a little peace and quiet, and found Costa Ilios to be the perfect balance of romantic isolation and proximity to town. Costa Ilios apartments rent for a minimum of seven consecutive days, June through September, ranging from $663 per week for a studio apartment up to $1,300 for a larger unit with separate bedrooms. For more information, call the Mykonos Accommodation Center at 011-30-289-23160 or 23408, or E-mail mac@mac.myk.forthnet.gr.

• • • • •

The major hurdle to eloping in Greece is the waiting period, which varies from island to island—even from town to town within the same island—as determined by the frequency of the local newspaper. Mykonos's paper is published once a week, which means that couples must arrive a full eight days prior to their wedding to announce their intentions, a requirement. We visited city hall in Mykonos Town in the hope of finding a loophole, but the registrar there was inflexible. What's more, the

Greek consulate in San Francisco had translated every word of our birth certificates, passports, and an affidavit attesting to the absence of any impediments to our marriage, but had left our proper names in English. This was the source of much consternation for the registrar. "I can take care of it," she said crossly. "But only if you are staying eight days."

Eight days we did not have. But a couple phone calls confirmed what had previously been rumored to us: one particular city hall on the island of Santorini was considerably more flexible. The registrar there, Ioannis (John) Kavalaris, invited us to pack a day bag and catch the next flight. "No problem," he said cheerily. "Don't tell Mykonos." We told him we'd need twenty-four hours to make arrangements and copied down directions from the airport to his office at Thira (Fira) City Hall, "above the cable car." This last bit didn't immediately make sense to us either.

Santorini is a volcanic island with black hills and black sand.

Somehow, Santorini was even hotter than Mykonos. From the airport, the deputy mayor's directions called for our driver to leave us "at the base of the gondola," a mode of uphill transportation usually associated with more Arctic climes. During our taxi ride, however, the reason for his choice of words became clear. All of Santorini is a dormant volcano, and the town of Thira perches spectacularly at the rim of the crater. The heart of the town connects with a harbor below via 587 windy steps. And a gondola.

At Thira City Hall we found our man, John, in jeans and a polo shirt seated amid a pile of papers at a gray desk (government-issue office furniture is the same color everywhere). At first, there was some confusion whether we were going to do the deed right there in the gondola stanchion; we even began to change from our grimy travel clothes into wedding togs. Then John announced it would take him a while to get the paperwork in order and offered to meet with us again after we'd freshened up at our hotel. We jumped at the offer—or should we say shuffled? By virtue of its precarious perch, the preferred mode of transportation within Thira is stairs. We set off for our hotel, luggage in tow.

Atop one especially shallow expanse of steep steps, the check-in desk for our hotel, Dana Villas, appeared as an oasis of air-conditioned calm. We collapsed in the small office, soaked in sweat. In the process of checking us into our rooms, the desk clerk, Dimitri, let slip that the hotel itself has been the site of dozens of wedding ceremonies. Snapshots from several of these events stood in a loose pile at the bar by the pool. Then we saw the view from the tile porch attached to our room, and the seed of an idea began to take shape: instead of us going to city hall to meet John, would John come to us? Lisa lunged for the phone. John, always agreeable, said yes without hesitation. Another phone call to Dimitri at the front desk secured a bouquet of yellow roses and matching

The view from our room in Thira; the perfect perch for a Santorini wedding ceremony

lapel pin. Hotel employees treat you kindly when you elope. It's one of the perks.

This left us several hours to loll by the pool, nap, and take in the view from our porch. Santorini is a major wedding spot. Travel agents throughout the island prominently display snapshots of ceremonies on their walls. Though we'd been on the island less than an hour, it was easy to see why: the scenery. From a distance of several hundred feet, the Aegean appeared beneath us as a solid pane of blue speckled with miniature cruise ships. Thira spread its whitewashed wings on either side of the cliff that surrounded our hotel. One hundred yards in the distance, a donkey stood tethered to a patch of grass among the stratified cliffs. No donkey in the world enjoys a better view.

We enjoyed an Amstel Lite by the pool and forked through a salad in search of our appetites. Prewedding jitters, combined with the heat, had sapped our taste for food all day. As the appointed hour approached, we retreated to our room to shower and change into our wedding clothes.

A rap on the door revealed John, briefcase in tow, now dressed in a sharp suit and wraparound shades. We recruited a hotel employee to serve the dual role of witness and photographer, rearranged the chairs on our deck to maximize our backdrop, and got married.

The ceremony was short and literally sweet—the prepared vows were especially touching. John was a pro; though he'd performed this ritual many times before, nothing felt perfunctory. A small crowd of fellow hotel-dwellers, who gathered by the pool to view our ceremony from below, erupted in applause when we kissed.

It's not unusual for brides to retain their maiden names in Greece, but there's a catch: couples have to determine on the spot what family name their children will inherit. Immediately after our ceremony concluded—indeed, so soon as to be considered part of the ceremony itself—John produced a document on which we were asked to ink our decision. Couples should negotiate an answer to this momentous question beforehand, unless they're prepared to hash it out beneath the deputy mayor's poised pen. Between us, it was decided that Lisa would write "Silverstein" on the document. As John secured the clasps on his briefcase, we provided him with an envelope containing our agreed-upon fee in drachmas (equivalent to U.S.$200) and a little something more to express our appreciation for his willingness to accommodate our every whim.

On Santorini, during the midday heat, there's no reason to linger in your warm wedding clothes. We were back in the pool

The deputy mayor was very accommodating. He not only performed our marriage with only twenty-four hours' notice, he also agreed to conduct the ceremony at our hotel rather than his sweltering office.

again within half an hour of our climactic kiss. The move sacrificed nothing in terms of the view.

That night, Dimitri directed us to the most romantic restaurant in town, Selene, and we were seated at an outdoor table with a sweeping view of Thira. Restaurant fare on Mykonos and Santorini is flavorful, but nothing fancy. A typical dinner comprises a deluge of small plates (the concept of courses is a foreign

The Vows

The script provided by Thira City Hall for our ceremony in Santorini was among the more touching and progressive we encountered anywhere during our year on the circuit. The man shall say:

> I take you, [name of bride], to be my wife, from this day forward. I promise before God and these witnesses to be your faithful husband, to join with you and to share all that is to come, to give and to receive, to speak and listen, to inspire and to respond, and in all circumstances of our life together to be loyal to you with my whole life and with all my being. I will love you as your husband, your lover, and your friend, so help me God, one day at a time.

Then the woman shall say the following:

> I take you, [name of groom], to be my husband, from this day forward. I promise before God and these witnesses to be your faithful wife, to join with you and to share all that is to come, to give and to receive, to speak and listen, to inspire and to respond, and in all circumstances of our life together to be loyal to you with my whole life and with all my being. I will love you as your wife, your lover, and your friend, so help me God, one day at a time.

Then if a ring be provided, it shall be given to the minister, who shall return it to the man, who shall then put it

upon the fourth finger of the woman's left hand, saying
after the minister:

I give you this ring as a sign of my love, knowing that
love is precious and fragile, yet strong. I give you this
sign of our love as an ever-present symbol of the
vows we have made here this day. I give you this ring
as I give you my love.

one) containing local seafood, or salads assembled from the massive vegetables that somehow spring from the rock-strewn terrain. Families strolled along the low-lipped stairs that connect Thira's myriad boutiques and public arcades, licking gelato and enjoying the cool air. Light from the shops stood out excitedly against the dark sky and cliffs. We worked our way slowly through a bottle of blissfully chilly white wine, soaked in the scenery, and relaxed.

Dana Villas is convenient with regard to its proximity to Thira City Hall and outstanding in its killer view of Santorini's famous cliffs and harbor. Rooms start at approximately $175. For more information, call the complex directly at 011-30-286-22566.

Elsewhere on Santorini

You're going to have to take our word on this one: Santorini is the best place to elope in all of Greece. There are fabulous wedding spots elsewhere in the republic—and Greek wedding consultants by the dozen available to help pull ceremonies together—but no place offers a combination of flexible laws and local wedding services on a par with Santorini.

Tsitouras Collection

The two ritziest hotels on the island are ideal wedding spots. The Tsitouras Collection is a group of five elegantly restored and architecturally distinct homes, each with a panoramic view of the harbor. Rooms range from $366 to $439 per night. For more information, call 011-30-136-22326.

Vedema Hotel

This hotel is a neoclassical villa set amid Santorini's inland vineyards, ten minutes outside of Thira. Many rooms have romantic canopy beds, and the wine bar and restaurant are superb. Rooms are in the $250 range, breakfast included. You can phone 011-30-286-81796, or fax 011-30-286-81798.

Nuts and Bolts

Where to Start

Wedding logistics in Santorini are fairly straightforward and entirely doable on your own. Though not required, it is smart to fax your translated documents and arrival dates to Thira City Hall in advance. Someone will alert you if there are any glitches or conflicts. The fax number is 011-30-286-22814; the phone number is 011-30-286-22231 or 23175.

For weddings not held at city hall, most hotels in Santorini are able to help with arrangements or can refer you to a reputable local wedding planner.

Mykonos is a less accommodating, though equally scenic, locale for eloping. For more information, call Mykonos City Hall at 011-30-289-22201, or fax 011-30-289-22229.

Travel Information

For nonsmokers, deplaning in Athens is not unlike being punched in the nose. But despite its shortcomings, Athens's international airport is conveniently serviced by nearly every major carrier. We flew Virgin Atlantic Airways from the United States to London and then on to Mykonos. Virgin's toll-free number is 800-862-8621. Olympic Airways networks Athens and the Cyclades and can be reached at 800-223-1226.

Legal Requirements

To obtain a marriage license, couples must provide their passports, original copies of their birth certificates, a certificate of non-impediment to marriage from their local registrar, and certified divorce papers or previous spouses' death certificates if applicable. *All documents must be translated from English into Greek.* Your local Greek consulate is the best place to have this done; if you have your documents translated by someone else, they will need to be certified by the consulate anyway. The Greek consulate in San Francisco charged $200 to translate our documents. Don't take this step lightly: the registrars on Mykonos and Santorini both were adamant about it.

The cost of a marriage license in Greece appears to be flexible. Thira City Hall on Santorini charged $200. Local wedding planners are likely to charge less for this step, but will jack up the cost of flowers, a cake, and so on.

Lead Time

Waiting periods vary from island to island and town to town in the Cyclades, depending on the frequency of the local newspaper. Mykonos's paper is published once a week, so you must arrive eight days before your proposed wedding day. Santorini is considerably more flexible for some reason. We arrived at noon and were married by 3 P.M.

When to Go

The best times to visit Mykonos or Santorini are the shoulder months (June and September) between winter and the high tourist season. During July and August, the islands choke with tourists—mufflers are not a big point of emphasis—and mainland Greeks attempting to escape the heat.

Additional Contact Information

To reach the Greek National Tourist Association office in the United States, call 212-421-5777.

Take Our Advice

One thing we did absolutely right: taxis. For what it would have cost to rent a vehicle (or less), we experienced fewer worries and greater flexibility—and tapped a font of local knowledge. Taxi drivers tipped us off to the best beaches, coffee shops, et cetera.

Whatever you do, resist the urge to rent mopeds. The Cyclades are buffeted by a constant breeze, capable of whipping two-wheelers around like stray napkins. Pothole-strewn roads and hurried European drivers add to the danger. Everywhere we went on Mykonos we saw fellow tourists with fresh scrapes on their elbows and knees, presumably from moped mishaps.

The much-advertised "high-speed ferries" that run between Santorini and Mykonos are no bargain when you figure the time it takes to stop at every port of call along the way. What we had imagined would be a brisk cruise—at a savings of approximately $60 over flying—instead was a five-hour below-deck grind. Spend the extra money on a flight and skip the agony.

Recommended Reading
Anything meaty. The Cyclades are all about sitting by the pool with a good book. If you've been looking for the opportunity to knock off Homer's *The Odyssey*, this is it.

Switzerland

Cost: $$$

Degree of difficulty: Moderate

First, the good news. Switzerland has been cultivating its reputation as a world leader in the tourist trade for hundreds of years now, and the standards of service here rank above or beside anyplace else in the world. Unfortunately, the country's reputation for being expensive is equally well earned.

Luckily, there are ways around this issue. The first trick is to stay in a small town instead of the big city. The second is to book your elopement as part of a package deal and enjoy a savings over the cost of each individual element reserved piece by piece. Lindenmeyr Travel, Ltd.'s Regensberg wedding packages hit the bull's-eye in both cases.

Chips Lindenmeyr's U.S.–based company books weddings in Regensberg, a tiny village about twenty minutes outside of Zurich, where $3,500 buys a legal wedding ceremony and three nights' lodging, including meals. Views of the quaint chalets and impressive mountains are free.

Regensberg is a tiny village, so small as to be deemed a hamlet by those who can distinguish between the two. One or two small stores, a baker's shop, a tiny restaurant, and a goldsmith's are all that's here—it's not at all touristy. For anyone who's inclined to miss the presence of discos and the like, Zurich is close at hand.

Regensberg, where the hills are alive with the sound of wedding bells
(Zürich Tourismus)

Weddings here offer plenty of opportunities for pastoral gaz-
ing. The short drive from Zurich to Regensberg traverses rolling
farmland, and quaint villages dot the Swiss countryside with the
ubiquitous Alps in the distance. The Rote Rose Hotel in which
couples are housed is a beautifully restored thirteenth-century
structure built into the city's walls. A three-room "dream suite"
is furnished with seventeenth- and eighteenth-century antiques, the
most prominent of which is a four-poster canopy bed that beck-
ons almost as strongly as the spectacular views of the Alps outside the window.

The Rote Rose takes its name from its gallery of works by rose
painter Lotte Gunthart. Couples who wed in Regensberg receive

a print of one of Gunthart's more appropriate pieces: a painting that compares a rose to a bride. In season, Gunthart's daughter provides personal tours of the hotel's gardens, which contain more than fifteen hundred species of these stunning and sweetly scented flowers.

The garden would seem an ideal wedding spot, but alas, civil ceremonies in Switzerland take place indoors at the registry office. In Regensberg, this setting is completely in character with the rest of the town's historic charms. Formerly part of a thirteenth-century nobleman's home, the registry is partially furnished with period antiques, lending an air of permanence to the proceedings. Additional floral arrangements for the bride and the room help formalize the occasion and are included as part of the package.

The ceremony itself is a brief affair, but the reception that follows at the Rote Rose is rich with small-town charm. Receptions generally are held in the "cellar" of the hotel—since the town is built on a hillside, the ground floor looks out over local vineyards. Chamber music plays gently in the background as the bride and groom, along with a few local folks they've likely accumulated along the way (even the judge has been known to come along), enjoy the atmosphere of the Rote Rose's original stone structure and fortify themselves with local wine.

Following the reception, the wedding couple is treated to a candlelit dinner with champagne at the Lowen Restaurant in Dielsdorf, a village about a mile away from Regensberg. The old-style architecture and typically Swiss cuisine (read, delicious) complete the day perfectly. Returning to the hotel—and that awesome four-poster bed—is an exercise in anticipation. The surrounding Alps peer through the blinds as they have for other couples in that same room for centuries.

Nuts and Bolts

Where to Start

Lindenmeyr Travel's Regensberg wedding package costs $3,500. The fee includes the ceremony and flowers, a small reception, three nights accommodation at the Rote Rose Hotel, help with the pre-travel/prewedding paperwork, breakfast and dinner daily, a photographer, and other special touches. For more information, contact Lindenmeyr Travel, Ltd., at 212-725-2807.

Travel Information

Zurich Airport, the nearest to Regensberg, is serviced by Air Canada, American, Delta, Swissair, and United. Though it is possible to get from Zurich to Regensberg by public transportation (the train stops in Dielsdorf, about a mile away), rental cars are strongly recommended. The added mobility lets you take day trips in the vicinity, including Rheinfall (Rhine Falls) and Stein am Rhein. Several U.S. car rental companies operate in Switzerland, including Budget, Avis, and Hertz. Note that many of the country's airports charge a tax of 12 percent of the total rental in addition to the 6 percent the government already charges, so it's often advisable to pick up your car from a downtown location instead.

Legal Requirements

Civil ceremonies are all that's required for a legal marriage in Switzerland. Religious ceremonies are performed afterward and are optional. To obtain a marriage license, you'll need birth certificates, passports, a notarized affidavit certifying your eligibility to marry and residency (Lindenmeyr Travel provides a form for this), indication of legal names to be used after the wedding, and certified copies of divorce or death certificates of previous spouses (if applicable). It is necessary to appear in person before the Regensberg registry to receive your marriage license. Lindenmeyr will help with all of these requirements.

Lead Time

Switzerland's residency requirement is just three days. The paperwork must be filed a month in advance of your wedding day, however.

When to Go

The Regensberg package is available from March to November (except in July). June and early fall (September and October) are ideal. Switzerland floods with tourists during the peak summer months.

Additional Contact Information

For additional activities and advice on traveling in Switzerland, contact Switzerland Tourism at 212-757-5944 or visit www .switzerlandtourism.ch.

Part II

Islands

You had to know this was coming. No serious (or lighthearted) book about eloping would be complete without swaying palms and sandy beaches, sunsets and the sound of crashing surf. Beyond Vegas, beach weddings loom largest in the public imagination when one thinks of eloping.

Not all islands are alike. Some are more remote than others—that's the most obvious difference. The proximity-to-home issue leads to other distinctions: islands nearest major U.S. populations (read, Miami) tend to be the most resort oriented. And resorts are very good at economies of scale. If the kind of calm that's born of efficiency is part of your vision of the perfect wedding, then the Caribbean is the place for you.

The farther afield you roam, the more local color tends to seep into the ceremony. In Bali and Fiji, both of which we visited ourselves, the volume of local color borders on sensory overload. Eloping here is thrilling—the very opposite of calm.

This section gives you just six options from among thousands.

Bali

Cost: $$$$

Degree of difficulty: Moderate

We're embarrassed to admit that we arrived in Bali knowing hardly anything about the local culture. The island has long tickled Westerners' fancies with its ability to soothe frayed nerves—that we were aware of. But during our first day at our hotel we believed this was a function of the island's natural attributes. The Four Seasons Resort Bali at Jimbaran Bay is situated at the hook end of a sweeping arc of fine sand protected by an offshore coral reef. On the day we arrived the waves broke meekly against our knees as we waded into the sea, and the shallow angle of the ocean floor and a blazing equatorial sun conspired to heat the water to a womblike degree. This was Bali, right?

Shame on us.

Warm water and fine sand are nice and all, but Bali's pacifist vibe emanates from its inhabitants, who practice their devotion in day-long pageants of prayer. It wasn't until we moved beyond the beach that we noticed how every inch of the island had been decorated with bright ribbons, umbrellas, and meticulously prepared offerings to the gods.

Given the island's widespread observance of religion, eloping in Bali is inevitably a religious experience, informed by the

*The volume of local color in a Balinese wedding borders on
sensory overload.*

celebratory sensibilities of the locals. It's also an excellent way to
see the Balinese genius for decoration in its full glory.

The Four Seasons at Jimbaran Bay has all the comforts of
home, provided your home happens to be a marble-floored pavil-
ion with a cavernous bathtub, heated outdoor shower, open-walled
dining area, and plunge pool with a carved volcanic sandstone
fountain. Adding to the already considerable sense of luxury is the
feeling of privacy. Each villa at the Four Seasons is walled off from
its neighbor on three sides. The plunging angle of the property on
which the hotel is built obscures onlookers' view from the fourth.
The surroundings are so luxe, it's not unusual for guests to spend a
week or more at the resort and never leave the confines of their villa.

Hindu Dharma 101

Bali stands out from its Indonesian neighbors like the trunk of a banyan tree that's been wrapped in yellow fabric amid a thicket of bamboo (not an uncommon sight on the island, as a matter of fact). The reason is religion. While the rest of Indonesia is overwhelmingly Muslim, Bali remains almost exclusively Hindu. Balinese religious tradition is distinct—more animist, less dependent on sacred texts and prescribed prayers—from forms of Hinduism practiced elsewhere on the planet, particularly in India.

Balinese Hindus believe in a central god, Sanghang Widi Wasa, who manifests himself in three forms: Brahma the Creator, Vishnu the Preserver, and Siva the Destroyer. Most Balinese pay strictest attention to Siva the Destroyer, because his presence is most dramatically felt through suffering and sickness. But Balinese Hindus also expend considerable energy worrying about a bevy of demon spirits whose job it is to wreak lesser degrees of havoc—to break pottery, for example, or to upset babies—in the earthly realm.

Both camps must be appeased. Every day on the island begins with ritualized offerings (meticulously arranged in freshly woven palm-leaf trays called *canang*) of flower petals, rice, grain, and other small treasures placed reverently by the locals at their family temples—and on the dashboards of their taxis, on paths and bridges, in restaurants, and so on. Revered gods receive their offerings on high altars, while demons' are placed on the ground. When visiting Bali, it's essential that you watch your step.

Balinese temples, like the family compounds, are open to the sky, presumably to make it easier for the gods to stop by for a visit during ceremonies. Attempts to quantify the total number of temples on Bali vary wildly. Suffice to say you'll see them everywhere, in the woods, in rice paddies, at your hotel. At a bare minimum, every village has three temples, and every family compound has a shrine of its own.

Public temples of regional importance swell with pilgrims during religious festivals. Visitors are largely welcome at temple ceremonies, but use your head. Ask permission of individuals before taking their picture, avoid

Temple ceremonies in Bali are joyous affairs, full of color, dance, and outward displays of reverence.

standing between worshippers and the direction in which they are praying, and never attempt to climb an altar or stand at a higher altitude than a priest. Local custom also dictates that all visitors wear a sarong when they enter temple grounds. (Shorts are a definite faux pas.)

Different temple compounds contain different structures, but every temple has a *padmasana*, or shrine, that represents the macrocosm: stone carvings of demons and dragons on the first floor, then something that depicts the world of man, topped with an empty seat for *surya*, the god of sun. Often a tiny umbrella is rooted in this top level, ostensibly for *surya*'s comfort. Every temple in Bali is *kaja*, oriented to face Gunung Agung, a ten-thousand-foot-plus active volcano in the central part of the island that's considered eminently sacred.

A night at the Four Seasons Bali at Jimbaran Bay will run you $525, excluding meals. Packages help soften the blow; four-night "Romance" packages start at $2,198 and include breakfast each morning, a dinner in your villa, and a massage session for each partner. For more information, contact 800-332-3442.

On our first morning at the resort we were awakened by a driving rain storm that transformed the thatch roof of our villa into an enormous snare drum. After breakfast we visited the U.S. consulate's office in Denpasar in order to obtain an affidavit of non-impediment to our marriage, a matter of providing our passports and filling out a simple form. Indonesian law requires that visitors obtain this document once they arrive in Indonesia—a major

The Four Seasons at Jimbaran Bay has all the comforts of home, provided your home happens to be a luxurious Balinese villa.

hurdle for nationalities that don't happen to have consulates on the island. U.S. citizens have it easy.

From the consulate's office it was a short stroll to Bali Weddings International HQ, where we met with proprietor Katrina Simorangkir, the island's resident wedding expert. Personable, Australian, married to a Sumatran (the story of her own wedding ceremony in her husband's village is one you'll have to hear her tell), Katrina has built Bali Weddings International into a multi-employee juggernaut since founding the business six years ago. During the high tourist season she handles as many as fifty weddings a month. When it comes to eloping in Bali, Katrina can honestly say, "I am the only person on the island who has all the answers."

Katrina collected our affidavit and sat down with us to discuss the particulars of our ceremony. She knew the potential hot spots by heart. The morning of our wedding, a local hairdresser and makeup artist would arrive at our villa to help us put on traditional Balinese wedding attire, which is quite involved. "Be sure to go to the bathroom before they start wrapping," Katrina insisted. "After you're done up, it's nearly impossible."

A legal wedding in Bali consists of two parts: a civil ceremony presided over by the local registrar and a religious ceremony. Protestantism is one of five religions recognized by the Indonesian government, Katrina explained, and the most convenient for visitors to claim. The minister will change the text of his remarks to fit with your beliefs if necessary.

The swimming pool at the Four Seasons at Jimbaran Bay seemingly blends into the sea.

We parted with a handshake—and then Katrina remembered one last thing we should discuss in advance. At the outset of the ceremony, the minister would ask us to hold each other's right hands. "I suggest you grab his hand with both yours," Katrina told Lisa. "If you just grab each other's right hand it appears as though you've just met, and that's not a good look for a wedding."

The morning of our nuptials, two women arrived at our villa bearing baskets under their arms. It was time for us to put on our makeup.

Lisa went first, receiving a heavy base coat that was paler than her natural color and a mark between her eyebrows in the shape of a tiny diamond bisected with a dark line. The mark, it was explained, represented the three major godly forces—creation, preservation, and destruction—that Balinese Hindus believe their deity possesses. The most powerful principle in Hindu dharma, or divine law, is balance.

Then came the hair. Lisa's natural locks were bundled tightly behind her head and fastened with a pin. To this was added an extra bun of fake hair for altitude. While one woman held all the hair in place, the second inserted a series of pins, each affixed with a single gold leaf, around the perimeter. The effect was colossal: after a hundred or so pins, the headpiece stood a foot and a half tall and weighed several pounds.

Lisa was now ready to be corseted and wrapped in a multi-layered crimson and gold sarong, *sabuk* belt, and tight *anteng* chest cloth. When this was done, the only unadorned area of her body was her feet.

Sam received pancake makeup in the same shade as Lisa's and a pair of elongated sideburns drawn on with eyeliner. Between his eyes was drawn a diamond-shaped mark similar to Lisa's, "for purity." On top of his head went a modest little crown. Each element of Sam's getup was a slightly less spectacular reflection of Lisa's, as if the object were to not overshadow her on her wedding day. At the last moment, one of the women thrust a kris dagger and sheath in the gap between the fabric of Sam's sarong and his shoulder blades. Though ceremonial, the dagger would serve nicely if anyone had something to say about his lipstick.

The Four Seasons has the perfect spot for outdoor affairs—a flat, shaded patch of grass on a natural terrace overlooking the bay. For our ceremony, the landing was transformed into a garden of hand-hewn delights. Palm fronds arced over the altar at calculated angles. Single marigolds dangled stems up from strings laced to the limbs of nearby trees. Balinese Hindus sprinkle umbrellas liberally around the grounds of their temples, to shield exalted gods from the sun or to add a whimsical touch to grotesque *paras* (carved stone demons) that exist closer to the ground. Yellow and blue umbrellas lined the path of our entrance, a flight of rock stairs that led from the sparkling pool down to our altar. As we descended into the fray, young girls in brilliant sarongs tossed flower petals at our feet. An elaborate gamelan orchestra seated on the ground kicked up a festive tune on a dozen or more tuned gongs, double-ended drums, and *gangsas*—xylophone-like instruments on which the musicians pounded out notes with tiny pickaxes then immediately dampened them with thumb and forefinger.

At the altar we were directed to stand—Lisa to the right, Sam to the left—before a table. The crimson-robed Protestant minister stepped forward to lead us through a brief religious service. As coached by Katrina, we clasped each other's hands

The Balinese genius for decoration. A simple grassy knoll was transformed into a fantastic garden for our ceremony.

The wedding party

intimately. We exchanged rings, repeated vows from a script, and signed our marriage certificate. While smooching, we had to be careful not to smear each other's lipstick.

The registrar then stepped to the fore to perform the civil ceremony, during which he listed four principles of marriage according to the Republic of Indonesia and "rights and duties" of the couple according to the law. Some of these were decidedly old world ("The husband is the leader of the family, and the wife is the mother of the household.") and needed to be taken with a grain of salt.

The kiss: Bali

A Balinese troupe performed traditional dances between each stage of our ceremony.

In addition to our civil and religious ceremonies, we also had asked that the Four Seasons arrange for a Balinese blessing ceremony presided over by a Hindu celebrant. For this, Katrina instructed us to sit. The orchestra struck up a rhythmic, energetic tune while three young girls sprang onto the scene from an unseen entrance. Their welcome dance was both choreographed and spastic: while they revolved around each other in slow, symmetrical formations, their fingers wiggled continuously and their necks clicked at asymmetrical angles in time with the music. When the orchestra kicked up a notch in intensity, the dancers' eyes widened in mock panic and darted left or right. Their sarongs were brilliant shades of gold and crimson, layered like ribbon candy.

On the heels of the dancers' youthful beauty, the Hindu celebrant's abrupt appearance was a shock. His mouth and eye sockets were sunken—caved in, really—with age, and the whiskers on his chin and upper lip were white. The celebrant did not smile or even acknowledge our presence, but said a few words of prayer beneath his breath and immediately began working through an elaborate pile of offerings stacked in baskets on the table before him. Everything about him communicated concentration. We sprang reflexively to our feet.

On our palms he rubbed fragments of burnt wheat cake, ground limestone, turmeric, and crushed flowers taken from the basket, then dipped his fingers in a Pyrex cup that was half-filled with water and pressed his hand against ours. The next item in the basket was a yellow dwarf coconut containing more water—blessed, presumably—into which he dipped a dried palm frond frayed like a buggy whip. He used the frond to sprinkle our faces, Pope-like, with aggressive little snaps of his wrist. Finally, the celebrant attached lengths of string to each of our forearms and slipped single frangipani blossoms beneath them; in his tradition, this signifies the beauty of our bond with one another. Only then did he extend his withered hand to us in a gesture we recognized as a handshake and offered the tiniest nod. It was enough.

Elsewhere in Bali

When it comes to eloping in Bali, Bali Weddings International has the island blanketed. So the question is not how, but where.

Amandari

At the top end for luxury and attentiveness, this resort is The Four Seasons' nearest rival on Bali. Located near Ubud, Bali's cultural and handicraft capital, Amandari recently received the highest approval rating of any property or destination in the world in

Condé Nast Traveler's annual Reader's Choice Awards. For more information, contact 800-637-7200.

The following boutique hotels and retreats all rent rooms for around $200 per night.

Ibah Hotel

This intimate resort, on the banks of the Campuhan River right in Ubud, features ten distinctly designed villas. There are great gardens and stoneworks, too. For information, call 011-62-361-974466, or fax 011-62-361-974467.

Linda Garland's Estate

Also in Ubud, this twenty-five-acre hideaway's private bungalows were featured on the cover of the March 1994 issue of *Architectural Digest*. More than twenty artesian springs gurgle within the property's boundaries, and the thirty-meter pool is spring fed. To find out more, call 011-62-361-974027, or fax 011-62-361-974029.

Waka di Ume Resort

Waka di Ume's allure lies in its location near Ubud, surrounded by serene rice paddies. A great place for total relaxation and meditation. You can call them at 011-62-361-96178, or fax 011-62-361-96179.

Damai Lovina Villas

Bali's northern highlands provide refuge from the tourist hordes that populate the island's southerly locales. If food is your thing, the restaurant here is headed by a French sous chef and the menu changes daily according to whatever's fresh. For more information, phone 011-62-362-41008.

Puri Ganesha

Four villas right on the beach in northwest Bali, Puri Ganesha is just five minutes away from some of the best diving on the island. The personable English proprietor works hard to showcase the region's culture. To get information, phone 011-62-361-261610, fax 011-62-361-261611, or E-mail novus@ibm.net.

Nuts and Bolts

Where to Start

Dealing with Balinese wedding logistics directly is nearly impossible. If you go through a hotel, they're going to subcontract with a local wedding company, Bali Weddings International, anyway. It's better to cut out the middleman and call BWI directly at 011-62-361-287516, E-mail them at baliwed@dempasar.wasantara.net.id, or see www.bali-paradise.com/baliwedding.

Bali Weddings International's handling fee for the legal wedding is $550. The company charges an additional $180 for couples who wish to wear traditional costumes (including the services of a dressing assistant) and $150 for help with their makeup and hairdos.

Travel Information

A dozen international carriers service Bali. We flew Malaysia Airlines from Los Angeles to Denpasar via stunning new Kuala Lumpur International Airport. For more information, contact Malaysia Airlines at 800-552-9264.

Legal Requirements

Indonesian law dictates that all marriages must be officiated by both a religious minister and the local registrar, in that order. Couples must identify themselves as Protestant, Catholic, Moslem, Hindu, or Buddhist. Protestant ministers generally do not require proof of religion and are the most willing to accommodate secular visitors.

Couples must obtain a certificate attesting to the absence of any impediments to their marriage from their consulate *within* Indonesia (U.S. citizens may obtain this document from the American Consular Representative in Bali at a cost of $55). For this certificate, they must present their passports as well divorce decrees or previous spouses' death certificates, if applicable. Couples also must provide six passport-sized snapshots of themselves together, which will be attached to their marriage certificates (so dress nicely). If you let this slide until the last minute, it's not a big deal to have passport portraits done in Bali.

Though not legally required, the opportunity to incorporate a Balinese Hindu blessing ceremony into your wedding is not to be missed. The Four Seasons Resort at Jimbaran Bay charges $300 to decorate the grounds and coordinate the gamelan orchestra, dancers, and priest. For more information, talk to the concierge when you make your reservation.

Lead Time
Bookings with Bali Weddings International made less than two weeks in advance are available according to demand, though subject to an additional $50 charge.

When to Go
Located eight degrees below the equator, Bali is tropically humid and hot year-round. November and December are marked by evening showers and thunderstorms that occasionally linger into the following day. They rarely last long, however, and are welcomed by the locals for their cooling properties.

July, August, Christmas, and New Year's are extremely busy. The Four Seasons Jimbaran Bay never feels cramped, however. The resort's architecture successfully absorbs people like a sponge.

Take Our Advice

One thing we did absolutely right was dressing up for our wedding. There's no prohibition against playing it straight; indeed, the majority of couples with whom Bali Weddings International has worked opt for the traditional somber suit and white wedding dress. But to truly absorb Bali's deeply spiritual vibe, it helps to walk a mile in the locals' shoes, or sarong as it were.

You might want to do a little research before you go. If we'd read up on Balinese Hinduism before arriving, we would have had a better understanding of the complicated drama that unfolds before visitors' eyes everywhere on the island.

Recommended Reading

To visit Bali is to understand the degree that Balinese architecture, art, and design has permeated all corners of the world. For a crash course, check out *Bali Style*, a coffee table book photographed by Rio Helmi with text by Barbara Walker. *The Flowers of Bali* by Fred and Margaret Eiseman is a pocket book you'll want to have in tow during your stay on the island. The flowers here are in-your-face interesting. *Bali: Sekala & Niskala* volumes 1 and 2, also by the prolific Fred Eiseman, comprise an encyclopedia of Balinese culture, with lively essays on topics ranging from *banjars* (village organizations) to betel root chewing.

Fiji

Cost: $$$$

Degree of difficulty: No sweat

American Richard Evanson came to Fiji in the early 1970s search-
ing for an isolated island on which to escape his demons. "I was
making a lot of money, drinking more, and enjoying it less," says
Evanson, an engineer by trade, of the years preceding his flight.
"And I was having health problems related to the drinking. I tried
a bunch of different things—self-improvement, went to a lot of
shrinks. Then I thought, 'I'll try buying an island.' That clicked."

For several years after he purchased and subsequently
renamed Turtle Island (also called Nanuya Levu), located in the
Yasawa Group of islands northwest of Viti Levu, Evanson and a
local villager, Joe Naisali, prettified the five-hundred-square-acre
property with frenzied plantings. The idea of opening Turtle Island
to the outside world, however, dawned over time. "After beauti-
fying the island, we decided it would be nice to have some people
around to share it with," Evanson says.

The process of transforming his private island into a vaca-
tioners' paradise was hastened in 1979, when a Columbia Pictures
film crew arrived to shoot a remake of *The Blue Lagoon* (the original, starring Jean Simmons, also had been shot on Nanuya Levu
thirty years previously). Facilities that were built for Columbia
Pictures' crew were incorporated into the resort, also named Turtle

Island, which received its first guests in 1980. The release of *The Blue Lagoon* later that year helped publicize Turtle Island (and fourteen-year-old Brooke Shields) internationally.

A legacy of the movie shoot is "Turtle Time": to help roust his crew out of bed each morning, the director had all the clocks on the island pushed ahead one hour. To this day Turtle Time helps cover for slipups—tardy seaplanes, slow days in the kitchen, et cetera—which are part of Turtle Island's charm. The resort has an accidental quality to it, as if elements of the guest experience have been invented from scratch. Because they have. "When we first opened, we didn't have but one table, so everyone sat together," Evanson says. "We didn't have time to get a liquor license, so I gave the booze away for free. And we came to find out that people liked it that way. It brings them together, makes them equals."

Indeed, people get chummy during their stay at Turtle Island. Resort staff refer to guests by name at first, then quickly bestow

Jean-Michel Cousteau Fiji Islands Resort is a diver's paradise.

(© 1994 Tom Ordway/JM Cousteau Productions)

nicknames on them that stick like glue. If you arrive with a quirk that can be exploited for comic effect—a distinctive laugh, say, or an excessive sunscreen habit—the staff will tease you without mercy. The distance between the guests is similarly compressed by communal meals, by volleyball games, and by the sense of being alone together on an island in the middle of the South Pacific that's roughly twice the distance from Los Angeles to Hawaii on the same trajectory. You are finally forced to admit that the best part of Turtle Island is not the white sand beaches, the swaying palms, or the clear water, but the party.

• • • • •

Our arrival at Turtle Island via seaplane from the mainland inspired a furious outbreak of singing, banner waving, and video-taping by the staff. Several couples who were scheduled to leave on the plane on which we arrived were among the throng that met us at the beach. "The food's good here, as you can see," said a Santa-shaped veteran, holding his belly. "Don't get burned on your first day. That's what my husband did," said another patron. "Be sure to bring an extra bottle of champagne on your picnics," a young honeymooner whispered conspiratorially. "It's impossible to get hungover on this island."

Turtle Island's summer camp first impression was reinforced by our initial tour of the grounds. A main reception area, sheltered dining hall, and communal table beneath an enormous banyan tree are the hub of the resort. Nearby, a stack of small sailboats, sea kayaks, and other toys were available for us to sign out at any time with the "dock lady," a staffer who sat in a shaded chair at the end of the resort's pier. The guest cottages fanned in either direction from this focal point along a picturesque strip of white sand—*The Blue Lagoon* incarnate.

If you prefer to play as part of a group, there's certainly plenty of that at Turtle Island. But couples who come here to indulge their own deserted island fantasy also are accommodated. At the extreme end of the spectrum are the beaches: the resort hosts no more than fourteen couples at a time, and there are fourteen distinct strips of sand on the island. Even when Turtle Island is booked solid (which it nearly always is), there are sufficient beaches for every couple to have one all to themselves.

We spent our first full day at Turtle Island on Honeymoon Beach, a one-hundred-foot stretch of powdery white sand framed on either end by cascading lava rocks. For shade, we faced a choice: a crude *bure* (cottage) with a hammock or three palm trees that cast their shadows on the beach. We chose the latter and lay on our backs in the sand, munching teriyaki chicken wings from a cooler, contemplating the consequences if a coconut were to drop on our heads. Then we marched into the water for a postmeal snorkel.

Dinner that night also was a private affair, served on a raft seventy-five feet or so off the dock. Later we rejoined the rest of the guests for a weekly Sunday night screening of *The Blue Lagoon*. Joe Naisali, who continues to work at Turtle Island as a social director of sorts, provided running commentary during the show. "That's a miracle baby," he cracked during a scene in which Brooke Shields's character gives birth. "Three weeks from start to finish." Later he sprang to the screen to point out himself and his cousin in a scene in which they appear.

Weddings are not only a cottage industry at Turtle Island, they're also a source of entertainment for the guests. While the movie's credits rolled, an announcement was made about our ceremony the next day. We returned to our *bure* for the night with butterflies in our stomachs, assured of a substantial audience.

• • • • •

Our wedding day began with measurements in the main office for floral headbands that would be made for us over the course of the afternoon. When we returned to our *bure*, we discovered that our bed had been decorated by the staff with palm fronds and hibiscus flowers.

At low tide, we joined an expedition to neighboring Matacawalevu for some clam digging. Our first few forays into the tidal mud were unproductive, until a villager who was working the same flat came by to offer assistance: if we used our feet instead of our hands, we could double our coverage and save our backs at the same time. She laughed at our first fumbling attempts to identify our prey with our toes, but seemed genuinely pleased when we started pulling clams from the mud with some regularity. (Our booty was served up as an appetizer that night.)

What remained of the day was occupied with tandem in-room massages and with interviewing the staff about the narcotic effects of kava, a mysterious potion that would be served at a ceremony immediately following our nuptials. Whenever the subject of kava is raised on Turtle Island, the always-jovial staff grows serious. Midafternoon, Joe pulled Sam aside and delivered a primer in kava protocol. When presented with a *bilo* (bowl) of kava, Sam should clap once as a sign of acceptance. Before putting the bowl to his lips, he should wait for all the attending groomsmen to clap three times. Then guzzle—kava is never sipped.

Fijian weddings traditionally take place at sunset. At 6:30 P.M. sharp, three women and a photographer arrived at our *bure* to help us dress in traditional Fijian garb for our ceremony. From a cardboard box the women produced several enormous panels of paper, thick enough to hold their skirtlike shape but slightly soggy and pliable in the humidity. These were our clothes, known as *masi* or tapa, pounded from the bark of a mulberry tree by nearby villagers expressly for weddings. Tapa cloth traditionally is decorated with red and black pigment set in geometric patterns and then left in the sun to darken. Ours were imprinted with repeat turtles, a nod to the resort's logo.

The attendants took us into two separate rooms, and wrapped the tapa panels around us sequentially. A wide skirt that fanned severely outward at our feet came first, followed by a middle section to cinch our tummies. Sam received a sash to cover his chest and one shoulder. Lisa wore a paper bra. We won't pretend that tapa was comfortable to wear (have you ever known anyone to voluntarily wear bark?), but it certainly was festive and nicely cool. The temperature throughout our stay in Fiji hovered in the high eighties.

While Lisa's attendants applied the finishing touches to her outfit, Sam was dismissed from the *bure* and instructed to make his way to a wall-less chapel one hundred yards down the beach. Here, about sixty staff and guests were seated beneath the thatched roof, facing each other on plastic chairs. Between them stood an altar.

Lisa's arrival was exponentially more dramatic than Sam's. From the direction of our *bure* was heard the blast of a conch shell, then there came a gentle splashing as a waterborne *billy billy* (raft) poled by three men in grass skirts rounded into view from the far end of the lagoon. When the raft had drawn even with the chapel, the men shipped their poles and linked their forearms in the shape of a chair, into which Lisa flopped and was carried ashore entirely

Lisa arrived on a billy-billy; Sam hoofed it, in bare feet no less.

dry. A staffer who had befriended Lisa was invited to serve as the maid of honor, a role she clearly relished. Andrew, a guest from New Zealand, stood as the best man.

Guests are serenaded morning, noon, and night during their stay on Turtle Island, and weddings are considered occasions for full choir performances. Our ceremony began with a hymn, then unfolded in alternating rounds of singing by the staff and sermonizing by a local minister, Reverend Josevata Vakatuturaga ("Reverend Joe"). The vast majority of indigenous Fijians are Methodist, and for our ceremony Reverend Joe wore a collar, sport coat, and white *sulu* (a

We all wore skirts, even Reverend Joe.

wraparound cloth worn like a skirt). Some of his directions were delivered in his preaching voice, meant to be heard by everyone in the chapel. Other times he whispered with us conspiratorially. He was adamant that we face each other and concentrate on connecting with our "eyes, hands, and spirits" throughout the twenty-five-minute ceremony. After a last hymn from the staff and a kiss between us, we made a rice-strewn retreat from the chapel.

The kava ceremony followed, for which the male staff arranged themselves in a crescent shape around a large *tanoa* (carved basin) and the women left the premises. We were directed to sit before the basin, facing the men. A staff member rose from the back to make a speech in Fijian, offering us his blessing and the kava as a symbol of respect. A second man murmured our 'response' by proxy, a gesture that is part of every kava ceremony regardless of language barriers. The kava powder, which smells

The kiss: Fiji

vaguely peppery and is the color of nutmeg (half-kilo plastic bags were displayed for sale in the hotel gift shop), was mixed with water in the basin. The staffer whose hands came in direct contact with the concoction during the mixing wore latex gloves to preclude numbness.

Then a staff member rose from his seat, dipped a bilo in the basin and approached Sam, who clapped once in appreciation per Joe's instructions and guzzled the contents in two gulps. The watery potion was gritty in texture and not unpleasant tasting, but far from familiar. It numbed the lips on contact. Lisa's offering was smaller and guzzled with equal aplomb. Our legs tingled pleasantly when we stood to leave, though whether this was a

The bride and groom are showered with rice in Fiji, no different than at home.

function of the kava or sitting cross-legged on the ground was unclear.

While each guest was offered a taste of kava, we returned to our *bure* to change out of our tapa outfits for dinner. The evening culminated with a meal at a long table on the beach, attended by our fellow guests and several members of the staff, including Joe. Sharing the table with friends whom we had accumulated during our stay added a homey touch to the day's events, and the meal

Kava

There is no analogue in our culture for the role that kava—a tranquilizing, nonalcoholic drink made from the powdered root of a local pepper plant—plays in Fijian society. Kava is served with great reverence at rituals such as weddings and funerals, as well as informally during office breaks and nightly card games. When we asked one of the managers at Turtle Island what we could do (in addition to leaving a tip) to express our gratitude to the staff, he instructed us to purchase a kilo of kava for their regular Saturday evening party. Among indigenous Fijians, kava seemingly is worth more than money.

Kava ceremonies are performed throughout Fiji, and attending a kava ceremony is de rigueur for any visitor. Ignoring the protocol associated with drinking kava is impolite at best, so take note. If you are offered kava, you must clap once before taking the bilo. After drinking the kava in one continuous motion, hand back the bilo and clap three times. If you are at all apprehensive, you can ask for a small bilo or, if you wish to decline, link your thumbs and place your hands gently on the rim of the bilo and push down. The only time you should clap during a kava ceremony is when taking your own bilo of kava or after another person sitting in front of the kava bowl finishes his or her bilo. Do not clap at any other time.

A few other don'ts:

- Never join the ceremony once it's in progress.

- Never step over the rope that extends from the *tanoa* (basin) containing the kava in the direction of the honored guests.
- Never speak unless spoken to.
- Never bring alcohol or any other intoxicant to a kava ceremony.

was marked by storytelling and boozy speeches. Everyone on Turtle Island is like family.

Toward the end of the meal, the staff marched a wedding cake to our table with unprecedented fanfare. They circled and chanted, wheeling the confection in and out of the lamplight like a matador tempting his bull with a cape. The display roused our suspicions—hijinks had been a major theme of our visit, and it was rumored that previous couples had been served with cakes in the shape of a ball and chain or fashioned from impenetrable coconut husks. But ours was straight-up passion fruit and mango mousse, with a dollop of banana ice cream for color. Everyone enjoyed a slice.

To cap off the festivities, we had arranged to sleep "out," in an exposed bed in a primitive *bure* on one of the private beaches. Joe picked up a lantern from the dinner table and walked us across a couple hundred yards of lava-rock-strewn shoreline at low tide to our temporary lodgings. We were nervous about the night alone, and during our walk the conversation turned apprehensively toward the topic of Turtle Island's resident snakes. "They're no problem," Joe said with bravado. As if on cue a black-and-white-striped sea snake appeared in the light of his lantern, retreating languidly among the rocks. Joe paused with the lantern while the snake backtracked into the shadows. "See," he commented. "It's afraid."

"That was a big one," Lisa said.

"That was a small one," Joe corrected, and howled with laughter.

Elsewhere in Fiji

To be married in a city hall anywhere in the islands is a waste—Fiji is all about clean air and water and abundant sun. Fijian weddings for visitors vary little from resort to resort, however. So it all comes down to where you wish to stay.

Jean-Michel Cousteau Fiji Islands Resort

Jacques's son's place is one of the premiere diving spots in the entire world. Aboveground it's also a magnificent, tasteful resort, run by the same company that owns fashionable Post Ranch in northern California. The wedding package is $1,300. For more information, call 800-246-3454.

Vatulele Island Resort

Vatulele Island is Turtle Island's twin—isolated and expensive—except for its Mediterranean architecture. The wedding package here is $2,000. For more information, contact them at 800-828-9146.

Nuts and Bolts

Where to Start

Turtle Island charges $2,200 for "grand" weddings, including transportation to obtain the wedding license in Nadi, photos, food, decorations, traditional tapa outfits, you name it. "Private" weddings—sans Fijian attire, attended only by the couple, minister, and two witnesses—are $1,100.

Rooms at Turtle Island start at $1,088 a night per couple, inclusive of everything you can imagine. The minimum stay is six nights. For more information, call 800-255-4347 or see www.turtlefiji.com.

Travel Information

Air Pacific, Air New Zealand, and Quantas all service the international airport in Nadi (pronounced "Nandi"). We flew Air Pacific, Fiji's national airline. Our return trip was a red-eye that crossed the international date line, meaning we boarded our flight in Nadi at midnight and arrived in L.A. at noon the following day—totally painless. For more information on Air Pacific, call 800-227-4446.

Turtle Island Airways connects Nadi and the Yasawas, including Nanuya Levu (Turtle Island). Note that the cost of round-trip air transportation between Turtle Island and Nadi ($1,380 per person) is not included in Turtle Island's fee.

Legal Requirements

To obtain a marriage license, couples must provide their passports, certified copies of their birth certificates, and certified divorce decrees or death certificates, if applicable. Our "special license" was issued in Nadi three days before our ceremony without resistance. Although there is no official residency requirement, Turtle Island's policy is to require that couples arrive at least three days in advance of their grand ceremony. Turtle Island policy is to perform only Catholic or Methodist ceremonies (with a large dose of local color, of course).

Lead Time

If there's an opening at Turtle Island, you can make your booking, travel, and be married all in the same week. But that's no small "if." The resort is in high demand year-round. A little flexibility will be rewarded handsomely.

When to Go

Southeast trade winds buffet Fiji from June through October, the best time of the year to visit. During the rainy summer months (December through April), intermittent, pleasant showers are common—violent tropical storms less so.

Additional Contact Information

The Fiji Visitors Bureau in Los Angeles can be reached at 800-YEA-FIJI (800-932-3454).

Recommended Reading

Each guest *bure* on Turtle Island is stocked with a copy of *Turtle Tales*, the story of Evanson's adventures on Nanuya Levu. Be sure to read your copy when you arrive; it explains a lot about what's going on around you. Also, *The Happy Isles of Oceania* by Paul Theroux is an itinerant traveler's opinionated account of touring the South Pacific by kayak.

Take Our Advice

Turtle Island's brochures boast of deserted beaches and ultraprivate accomodations—amenities that do indeed exist. But the vibe here is decidedly social, to a degree that can catch the uninitiated by surprise.

The British Virgin Islands

Cost: $$$$

Degree of difficulty: No sweat

Eloping in the British Virgin Islands (BVI), a fifty-nine-square-mile vector of the Caribbean that comprises between forty or sixty islands depending on your definition of the term, is distinctly less willy-nilly than in some places. The phenomenon is explained in part by osmosis: this is hammock country, a sun- and humidity-saturated network of volcanic islands with a magical ability to loosen joints and empty cluttered minds. It's worth visiting this corner of the world just to see how people walk, especially the women. Their strides are unhurried and relaxed like cooked spaghetti.

On board a boat in the BVI, it's especially hard to get uptight about anything having to do with calendars or clocks. Even though we were scheduled to meet a wedding coordinator from Peter Island Resort at 10 A.M. sharp—and the amount of time it would take us to sail from our mooring to the designated meeting place was unclear—our thirty-eight-foot catamaran was devoid of punctuality angst. From a perch above the galley, we watched the shoreline slide by and contemplated the homes' eclectic architecture.

Deadman's Bay: an unfortunate name for such a pretty place
(Courtesy of Peter Island Resort)

This quickly gave way to an uncontrollable urge for sleep, which we did not fight.

From a number of upscale BVI resorts that offer wedding packages, we had chosen Peter Island Resort at which to tie the knot. The resort's wedding coordinator, Denise Hewlett, was napping in her Land Rover when we eventually arrived at our meeting spot. We were armed with our passports, birth certificates, and enough cash to knock off some paperwork in the BVI's local capital, Road Town, Tortola.

The British Virgin Islands being, after all, British, our first errand was to visit the central post office in Road Town and purchase the proper stamps. The quaintness of the exercise would have been amusing except for its steep price (U.S.$110) and the office's unwillingness to accept credit cards. We forked over the cash while a woman behind the counter leafed through sheets of colorful stamps. When she landed on the appropriate page, she carefully tore out a patch of wedding stamps, wrapped them in paper to protect against the humidity, and handed them to us. Out we went again into the midday sun.

Our second stop was the Registry of Births, Deaths, and Marriages to schedule our appointment with the registrar who would perform our ceremony. For this, we paid another $100 cash. Tourists usually must establish three full days' residency before a wedding ceremony may be held, but we were allowed to shorten the wait by a day with a minimum of scolding.

Third stop ("I'm telling you, the British system sometimes is a bear," said Denise) was the attorney general's office in the central administration building in Road Town, a serious-looking structure with a fountain in the lobby and the most aggressive air conditioning we encountered anywhere in the BVI. Here we applied for a marriage license and surrendered our colorful stamps and passports for verification. The island authorities take these things seriously; our passports would be scanned via computer to be sure no obstacles to our marriage existed. "The attorney general herself runs the passport numbers through her computer," Denise announced with pride.

Denise dropped us back at the marina where we had tied up for the day. We went to a public shower at the marina to freshen up—a relative term since, unaccustomed to the humidity, our skin broke a fresh sweat within moments. The ground seemed to sway beneath our feet. Finding our sea legs would require a full twenty-four hours.

• • • • •

The three-day waiting period provided an ideal excuse for exploring the territory by boat. Our hosts for the week were three friends from San Francisco—Karen and Carl, and their eighteen-month-old daughter Zoë—who had arrived a week before us and chartered the catamaran. The scenario offered us the best of all worlds: camaraderie and privacy, leisure and activity in pleasantly spaced intervals. Carl is an excellent sailor who was happy to handle all the heavy lifting by himself, but we were welcome to lend a hand when the spirit moved us. It was going to be an excellent week.

Our arrival the night before had provided time for only cursory inspection of the boat. Carl had anchored within walking distance of the landing strip in Tortola where our American Eagle island-hopper had set down. We had toasted our arrival over champagne and then turned in for the night, entirely pooped. The hypnotic slap, slap, slap of waves against the fiberglass hull in which our beds were located shortened the amount of time it took us to fall asleep to a nanosecond.

Now, while Carl kibitzed with the harbormaster at the marina, we had time to examine our floating home, the *Blue Moon*, more closely. The French-built catamaran's defining feature was twin hulls that connected at their midpoints to create an ingeniously space-efficient deck. Each hull contained two sleeping bays with room for a couple in each. Conceivably, the boat slept eight. A narrow hallway with a combination bathroom/shower connected the forward and aft bays in both hulls.

Where the hulls joined was a well-appointed galley with a gas stove, refrigerator, table, cabinets, and enough counter space to hold a dish-drying rack and a week's supply of those supermarket cookies that are perfectly not-too-sweet to eat all day long. Aboard the *Blue Moon*, every available inch of enclosed area was maximized. Bench seats with removable covers held troves of canned food, maps, and books.

The galley platform extended through a pair of sliding doors into the open air. Here was where the captain's chair stood, as well as a sun tarp–protected table and benches and a swimming pool (really a laundry tub) the size of a manhole in which Zoë spent part of each day surrounded by a small ecosystem of plastic toy animals. Shade proved to be a precious commodity right off the bat. Our first task on our first full day on board, after removing our watches and shoes, was to slather half a drum of SPF thirtysomething lotion on our pasty wintertime skin.

Our appointments met and the kitchen stocked with provisions, it was finally time to loaf in earnest. Carl prepared the *Blue Moon* to set sail, lashing our dinghy to the back rail and readying various lines and canvas sails. We made one standing offer to help Carl any time he needed us, then retired to a flat spot on the deck above the galley with a stack of postcards. The throb of the motor under us as we eased out of the marina was jarring at first. Soon, however, Carl cut the engines, raised our mainsail, and pointed us downwind. Our Caribbean vacation was under way.

The Blue Moon, *our floating hotel for the week*

• • • • •

The first part of our wedding day was spent facedown in the water examining fish through our snorkeling masks—a decidedly more pleasant way to spend the morning than worrying about no-show florists or grandmothers in their hotel rooms. The fish in this part of the world are colorful like exotic birds and equally abundant. A more fastidious couple than ourselves can inventory the tropical species of the British Virgin Islands with scientific accuracy. We were content just to follow them around as they nibbled coral reefs and cruised expanses of sea grass.

In the early afternoon, we made the short sail to Peter Island and tied up to a dock at the resort. The resort comprises the entire island, of which only a small area has been developed. Adding to Peter Island's allure is its architecture: more than half of the resort's fifty-plus guest rooms are incongruous A-frames imported from Norway and then reassembled on the site.

We met Denise in her air-conditioned office, where she walked us through a blow-by-blow itinerary of the day ahead. She had the proceedings scheduled to the minute: vows, then pictures, then dinner. In Road Town earlier in the week, we had developed a list of amenities we wanted for our ceremony. Per our directions Denise had procured a bouquet and corsage, matching flowers for Karen and Zoë, and color film for the photographer. We literally had nothing to worry about.

We checked into a room to shower off the sand, sun, and snorkeling residue and changed into our wedding clothes. At the appointed hour a knock on our door revealed Denise in a high state of excitement. The registrar, Helen Ali, followed close on her heels. Carl, Karen, and Zoë waited for us on the beach—a 200-foot walk, tops. The spot we'd chosen for our ceremony was a boardwalk overlooking Deadman's Bay, named for a group of mutinous crewmen whom Captain Blackbeard is said to have jettisoned on a nearby cay with only a single sword and a bottle of rum for sustenance. It's an unfortunately gruesome name for a pristinely pretty place; a half-moon of white sand on the wind-protected side of the island provides perfect mooring conditions for a handful of boats. Beyond the boats were blue water, vast horizons, and the occasional float plane or pelican. The sun ducked pleasantly behind a cloud for our ceremony.

After all our tightening of ties and futzing with hair braids, the wedding itself was a snap. Helen read from our wedding certificate and then said a few words of her own while a photographer snapped furiously; he'd worked this beat before and knew the window of opportunity was brief. The only glitch was that our fingers had swollen in the heat, making it difficult to exchange rings. (Note: pinky fingers are convenient substitutes in a pinch.) Within moments of our entrance, Helen pronounced us man and wife and invited us to seal the deal with a kiss. A series of photo opportunities ensued, with several scenic perspectives from which to choose. Us with the beach and the boats in the background. Us with just sand and water. Us with a garden and flowers.

With the moment sufficiently documented, we all piled into a golf cart to reconnoiter in a private dining room off the resort's main courtyard over canapés and champagne. The room had been decorated for the occasion with ribbons and a staggering number of fresh flowers. Place settings for each of us—featuring a satchel of candied almonds tied with a ribbon on each plate—foreshadowed the delicious dinner that was in the offing.

Helen broke out two copies of our wedding certificate for all the principals to sign. One certificate was for her to take with her back to Tortola. The other was ours to keep, preserved in a manila envelope stamped On Her Majesty's Service. A joking suggestion that Helen had misspelled Carl's name on the certificate almost killed her. Must be a British thing.

• • • • •

We slept late in our hotel room the following morning while Carl, Karen, and Zoë zonked on the boat. Then we reunited on the beach at Deadman's Bay around noontime. Peter Island Resort guests have free run of the activities shed; Carl signed up for a Hobie Cat—sort of a miniature rendition of the *Blue Moon*—and

No cell phones here
(Courtesy of the British Virgin
Islands Tourist Board)

spent a couple adrenalized hours criss-crossing the bay and slaloming among the anchored boats. We found side-by-side beach chairs and covered ourselves with sunscreen and towels to protect against the wind-whipped sand.

The week ended with one last glorious sail downwind from Peter Island to Tortola. All of the sounds associated with sailing are relaxing: water cleaving against the bow, wind against the sail, the tinkle of ice in our rum and tonics. With our twin hulls planing evenly over the top of each wave, the term "smooth sailing" suddenly made much more literal sense. We made extraordinary time in the stiff breeze, not that anyone was in a hurry.

Everywhere we went in the BVI we heard music. Peter Island's PA system had spilled out tunes from the poolside bar toward the resort's dock, where it clashed with radios on board the yachts. At the Soggy Dollar Bar on Jost Van Dyke, we had heard the *ragga* preferred by the locals. Here the soundtrack for our arrival at Soper's Hole Marina on Tortola's West End was provided by an ice cream boat that was working the assembled yachts. The ice cream boat warbled its invitation across the water, with a distinctly Caribbean twist—the tinny Wurlitzer we grew up with in the States had been replaced by a recorded steel orchestra.

Yachting 101

Sailing in the British Virgin Islands has more in common with tailgating than with the America's Cup. There's enough land around to soften the ocean's punishing swells without interrupting the steady and predictable fifteen- to twenty-knot easterly trade winds that once were the Caribbean's meal ticket. Add to this ample unspoiled anchorages, a community of yachtsmen, and huge yachting supply stores, and you're talking about a sailing mecca.

Wannabe yachtsmen have a variety of options to choose from based on expertise, energy level, and expense. Neophytes can charter a boat and crew at any number of marinas, then spend their vacation nibbling on prepared meals and coiling an occasional line or two when they feel like it. So-called "crewed" yachting is the sport in its most indulgent form. Chartering a crewed boat provides all the bang of a yachting life, with none of the effort—or mortgage payments.

Experienced sailors have the option of "bareboating," in which you choose your yacht from a roster of candidates and then sail it yourself. Most charter companies offer a range of options depending on price, ambition, and the size of your party. Larger yachts can accommodate a dozen or more people.

Caribbean-based charter companies abound. With nearly three decades in the yacht charter business, The Moorings is perhaps the most established outfit. For more information, call 800-535-7289 or see www .moorings.com. Sunsail is equally huge and can be reached at 800/327-2276 or www.sunsail.com.

The Catamaran Company specializes in multihulled boats, which are more stable in rough water and more spacious under any conditions. The company also employs a captain who is authorized to perform legal weddings. You can call them at 800-296-KATS (800-296-5287) or see www.catamaransailing.com. Nicholson Yacht Charters also offers weddings at sea (phone 800-662-6066).

Regency Yacht Vacations (800-524-7676), Sailaway Yacht Charter Consultants (800-724-5292), and VIP Yacht Charters (800-524-2015) specialize in crewed yacht charters. Bareboating is Caribbean Yacht Charters' area of expertise (800-225-2520).

If you're bareboating, don't dare hoist your anchor without a copy of *The Cruising Guide to the British Virgin Islands* on board. The guide features maps and invaluable insider information for enjoying each destination. It is available throughout the BVI or by calling 800-330-9542.

At Beef Island Airport, a mama goat and newborn kid occupied a patch of grass adjacent to the terminal. They wandered the grounds unbothered, though the mom clearly was on the lookout while the kid—umbilical cord still attached—was entirely carefree. The tourism board itself could not have imagined a more fitting farewell committee.

Elsewhere in the British Virgin Islands

Some BVI locales are livelier than others, some are more developed for tourists, but all make their bread and butter off of clear water, clean beaches, and abundant sun.

Necker Island

For the price of a tasteful wedding at a nice hotel—let's toss in salmon entrées and an ice sculpture, for argument's sake—you can have a slice of the jet-set lifestyle at Necker Island. The seventy-four-acre land mass, on the northeastern boundary of the British Virgin Islands, is entirely owned by Richard Branson of Virgin Atlantic Airways fame. Originally it was his own playground. Now it's available to rent, one party at a time.

The resort features three luxurious homes designed in the airy Balinese style and built with a combination of local stone and timber; Brazilian ipe; Yorkshire flooring; and specially commissioned furniture, fabrics, sculptures, and paintings. Each structure has its own swimming pool, and every room has an ocean view.

Richard Branson's personal paradise, Necker Island, is available for weddings—at a price. (Dougal D. Thornton)

There is no end to the list of things to do on your own private island. Games on floodlit tennis courts, scuba diving, deep sea fishing, sailing, excursions to nearby islands, beauty treatments, tennis, walking, windsurfing, waterskiing, and sailing all are included in the cost of renting the resort. Eating is the preferred pastime. Guests have at their disposal a twenty-two-member staff that includes several private gourmet chefs who specialize in elegant island food.

Renting Necker Island with one to seven guests costs $14,000 per day (that's $70,000 for five days). The only difference between renting Necker Island for kicks or for a wedding is the cost of obtaining a marriage license and a registrar to perform the ceremony. All other expenses are built into Necker Island's day rate, including the use of all three houses, gourmet meals and drinks, sporting equipment, and transfer from Virgin Gorda or Beef Island airports. Rent the place for a full week and Branson will provide a live calypso band for your wedding gratis. For more information, call 800-557-4255 or 212-696-4566.

Biras Creek

Although technically not a desert island, Biras Creek often feels like one. Located in a 140-acre peninsula on the North Sound area of Virgin Gorda, Biras Creek is accessible only by boat. Guests can arrange to be marooned on an empty beach for a day, then be picked up in time for a lobster dinner and some calypso music. Honeymoon suites feature sweeping views of the churning Atlantic. This is an intimate resort with thirty-three suites and a seaside freshwater swimming pool. Rooms range from $425 to $770, depending on the season. All food is included (but not drinks), as is use of the resort's water-sports equipment.

Wedding sites vary. Popular options include a private beach at Deep Bay, the balcony of Pelican Point Villa, or the deck of the

Biras Creek, on a peninsula on Virgin Gorda, is accessible only by boat.
(Courtesy of Biras Creek)

resort's luxurious yacht. Biras Creek's basic wedding package includes the marriage license and stamp fee, the registrar's fee, floral arrangements, a wedding cake, a champagne toast, and a photographer for $1,000. A videographer, live music, fireworks, printed napkins, and decorations can be added at an additional cost. For more information, call 800-223-1108.

Little Dix Bay

Voted one of the top twenty-five tropical resorts in the world by *Condé Nast Traveler* magazine, Little Dix Bay at the south end of Virgin Gorda is a sure bet for a luxurious beach wedding and honeymoon. Now more than thirty-five years old, "Little Dix has withstood the test of time by preserving the essence of what a relaxing respite in the islands is supposed to be all about," says exclusive vacation expert Andrew Harper.

Weddings at Little Dix Bay usually are performed on the beach or at a grassy verge overlooking the water shaded by

Peter Island Resort's incongruous A-frames are the first thing visitors see when they arrive at the marina. (Courtesy of Peter Island Resort)

bougainvillea. For more information, call 800-928-3000 or see www.rosewood-hotels.com.

Nuts and Bolts

Where to Start

Peter Island was developed in the 1960s by a wealthy Norwegian shipper. The Amway Hotel Corporation purchased the facility in the late 1970s and has operated it ever since. The resort underwent a major face-lift following Hurricane Hugo in 1997 and was hit hard again by Hurricane Georges in 1998.

Today it comprises fifty-two guest accommodations and three villas on eighteen hundred acres, including five distinct beaches. Rooms start at around $500. Fancy options include the Crow's Nest Villa, on the pinnacle of a hill with views of Tortola and beyond. The villa comes complete with designated staff, a swimming pool, and a golf cart for wheeling around the island. But it's not cheap; a night at the Crow's Nest costs in the neighborhood of $5,000 during the high season (winter).

Our Peter Island Resort wedding bill totaled $1,234. This included our photographer and three rolls of film ($480), bouquets and corsages ($101), champagne ($68), wedding cake ($75), coordination fee ($250), and miscellaneous expenses ($260). The coordination fee was for Denise's assistance with the details of the day and a total bargain. The package price does not include the cost of a marriage license ($110) and the registrar ($100). For more information, call Peter Island Resort at 800-346-4451, or visit www.peterisland.com.

Travel Information

Several major carriers service the Caribbean, but American Airlines (American Eagle, really) appears to have the place especially wired. For more information, call 800-433-7300.

Legal Requirements

A marriage license in the British Virgin Islands takes three working days to process upon your arrival. You'll need proof of identity—passports or certified copies of your birth certificates—and a photo

The Crow's Nest is a step up—literally and figuratively—from the rest of Peter Island Resort. (Courtesy of Peter Island Resort)

ID. Divorcees must have certified divorce decrees. Those who are widowed must have their late spouse's death certificate.

Lead Time

Peter Island Resort doesn't need any advance notice beyond the three days required by BVI law.

When to Go

Wintertime, of course. It's always nice in the Caribbean, so you might as well visit the British Virgin Islands while the place you're supposed to be is inhospitable. The off-season (June through November) offers less crowds and reduced rates, but a greater risk of having your vacation ruined by a wayward hurricane, which is no small thing.

Additional Contact Information

For general information about travel in the British Virgin Islands, contact The British Virgin Islands Tourist Board at 800-835-8530.

Take Our Advice

Weddings are more of an industry here than most places, and the locals can give off a "been here, done that" vibe. Look at the flip side of the coin: it's liberating to have confidence that the mechanics are going to come off like clockwork.

Recommended Reading

Fritz Seyfarth's *Tales of the Caribbean* is an organic little collection of sketches and short stories that comes off more like a slide show than literature—appropriately breezy fare for a sailboat.

Jamaica

Cost: $$$

Degree of difficulty: No sweat

Sandals's network of Caribbean resorts is an excellent tack to take if you want to go the pure convenience route. Here, literally every detail is attended to from the moment you arrive—from the moment you board the plane if you fly Air Jamaica, Sandals's official carrier. Sandals resorts are wedding factories, with ceremonies staged four times daily, including sunset. To say they've got their chops down would be a vast understatement.

Sandals's niche in the resort market is to offer guests the opportunity to frolic in the sun without having to carry their wallets. Sandals operates ten resorts in all, spread over four Caribbean islands. Jamaica alone houses four. Among them, Negril—which spans one of the island's most beautiful beaches—has proved particularly popular with eloping couples and honeymooners for its "slightly wicked" vibe. There are lots of nooks and crannies on the grounds, ideal for stealing a private moment away from the organized throng of fellow vacationers.

Sandals is a package deal to the bone: meals, booze, and all activities are included in one price, which ranges from $2,740 to $3,600, depending on your taste in room category, length of stay, and other factors. Sandals "WeddingMoons" are an additional $750, including all the trappings.

So it's a trade-off. You lose some freedom; so-called "all-inclusive" resorts are notorious for channeling their guests within the grounds of their property to the exclusion of the surrounding countryside. At Sandals, this is elevated to a science. The resort operates six compounds on the island of Jamaica, and guests are free to "stay at one, play at six." The brochure goes so far as to boast that it's possible to "savor the flavors of the world's greatest cuisines" without ever leaving the resorts' bounds.

But it's a good value, and eloping here is a total breeze. If you decide to make choices regarding your ceremony, you can. Upon arrival, a wedding coordinator will escort you around the property to display various options for wedding spots. The cake, flowers, and other details also can be tweaked if you wish. Or not. Many couples leave the details of their wedding to their coordinator and expend their energy on the amenities.

Sandals Resorts' all-inclusive fee buys ample sand, surf, sports, and sunshine.

(Courtesy of Sandals Resorts)

Located on a hefty chunk of Jamaica's famed seven-mile beach, Sandals Negril offers windsurfing, waterskiing, snorkeling, and scuba diving. Squash, racquetball, and tennis courts are part of an elaborate sports complex on the property, as are three fresh-water swimming pools. Regarding the sea kayaks, popular lore says that if a couple can manage to paddle together, they will manage to live together. Happily. Note that the all-inclusive fee also includes instruction.

Elsewhere in Jamaica

There are hundreds of alternative hotel wedding options on the island. Here are two that are the eloping friendliest.

Half Moon Golf, Tennis and Beach Club

This four-hundred-acre colonial-style resort in Montego Bay can feel like a small city. There's a shopping center, three restaurants, a pub, a bank, a doctor's office, a conference building, a 72 par golf course, tennis and squash courts, two freshwater pools, a Nautilus gym, and an equestrian center. Couples in search of an intimate experience may rent their own two-story villa with a private pool, maid, and butler. Half Moon also has 280 tastefully decorated rooms and suites.

Weddings at Half Moon take place in a gazebo surrounded by ocean. A glistening white sand beach or tropical garden also are options. Half Moon's standard wedding plan includes a marriage officer, a bottle of champagne, a bridal bouquet, a boutonniere for the groom, a wedding cake, a professional video, one roll of thirty-six pictures and negatives—all for $750. Couples can add embellishments such as horse-drawn carriage rides or floral and plant decorations at the wedding gazebo for an additional cost. Requisite wedding-day beauty treatments and massages are available on the premises. For more information, call 800-626-0592 or 876-953-3244.

Round Hill

Round Hill is a tidy little nest located on a ninety-eight-acre former sugar plantation. The resort cascades past stately palms and magical gardens down to its own pristine beach. Many of Round Hill's secluded villa suites have their own swimming pools. Activities include waterskiing, windsurfing, sailing, snorkeling, golf, tennis, and deep-sea fishing.

Most couples tie the knot in their bare feet on the crescent-shaped beach. Weddings also can take place in your own villa or in one of the resort's gardens overlooking the sea. Round Hill's wedding plan includes the cost of the marriage officer's services, a bottle of champagne, the wedding cake, a bridal bouquet, a photographer (and the cost of developing the prints), and a video—all for $700. For more information, call 876-956-7050 or 800-237-3237.

A master suite at Round Hill, in Jamaica   (Courtesy of Round Hill)

Nuts and Bolts

Where to Start

Sandals's basic WeddingMoon package is $750 and includes the services of a wedding coordinator and justice of the peace, help with the paperwork and legalities, a video, a half-hour massage for the bride and groom, a wedding reception in a decorated area with champagne and hors d'oeuvres, a two-tiered Caribbean wedding cake, a candlelight dinner for the bride and groom, a continental breakfast in bed the morning after the wedding, flowers, and other accoutrements. For more information, call 800-SANDALS (800-726-3257), or see www.sandals.com.

Travel Information

Air Jamaica is Sandals's official air carrier. For more information, call 888-452-6247. In addition, several major carriers offer daily direct and connecting flights to either Norman Manley International Airport in Kingston or Donald Sangster in Montego Bay. Sandals can arrange private car transfers to and from either airport.

Legal Requirements

You'll need to provide birth certificates and complete a wedding information form. You'll also need the following documents, if applicable: a final divorce decree; name change or adoption papers; parents' written consent (if either of you is under eighteen); legal translations of any foreign documents to English; and/or a late spouse's death certificate.

Lead Time

Sandals requires that its guests arrive in Jamaica a minimum of twenty-four hours before they tie the knot. The resort also requests that couples submit notarized copies of the required documents thirty days in advance of their wedding to the Miami office (4950 S.W. 72nd Ave., Miami, FL 33155), though this hurdle can be bypassed if a couple wishes to elope. For more information, call 800-327-1991.

When to Go

Northeast trade winds provide Jamaica with year-round natural air conditioning. Tourists flock to the island between November and April (spring break is chaos), but once you're within the bounds of Sandals Resort the outside world doesn't really matter. Jamaica is subject to hurricanes between June and November, and it can rain—typically short bursts of tropical showers—April to May and September to October.

Additional Contact Information

Call 800-JAMAICA (800-526-2422) for a free travel kit. The Jamaica Tourist Board also operates several regional offices in the United States. For the Northeast, call 212-856-9727; Midwest, 312-527-1296; West Coast, 213-384-1123; and South, 305-665-0557. The official website of the Jamaica Tourist Board is www.jamaicatravel.com.

Antigua

Cost: $

Degree of difficulty: No sweat

Christopher Columbus discovered Antigua on his second voyage in 1493. At first, because the island lacked an abundant supply of fresh water and fierce Carib Indians were less welcoming to outsiders, few colonial powers were interested in establishing a permanent presence on this 108-square-mile territory or its sister island to the northeast, 62-square-mile Barbuda. It wasn't until 1632 that the English claimed Antigua for the Crown.

English settlers on Antigua eventually figured out how to grow sugarcane successfully despite the island's dry climate, and other colonial powers began to covet the island's prosperity as well as its military advantages. Antigua, the northernmost Leeward Island, served as a naval base for English ships arriving in and departing from the Caribbean, and natural harbors here saved ships from the ravaging hurricane winds. Sailors still follow their compasses to Antigua's Sailing Week, held every April at Nelson's Dockyard. The diving here also is prime—not all Antigua's ships found safe harbor, and the ocean floor is littered with intriguing wrecks.

· · · · ·

Galley Bay's thatched-roof cottages remind one of Tahiti.

(Courtesy of Galley Bay)

The Copper and Lumber Store overlooking Nelson's Dockyard is a quirky Georgian inn that's soaked with history—an excellent elopement spot. The Store was erected in 1783 when shipbuilders discovered that copper could effectively protect the bottoms of wooden ships in tropical waters. However, with the modernization of vessels and the advent of peace, the property fell into neglect.

In 1950, a restoration project turned the Copper and Lumber Store into Antigua's most authentic, intimate inn. Unlike larger, more modern and generic properties on the island, the Store possesses unique charm. A weather-beaten figurehead in light blue greets guests at the door. Antique furnishings, old sailing prints, steamer trunks, original interior and exterior brick walls, polished wood floors, and four-poster canopy beds add to the colonial vibe.

Weddings at the Copper and Lumber Store are simple, low-key affairs officiated by a marriage officer from nearby St. John's, Antigua's capital. After a champagne toast, couples slip quietly into a corner of the dining room for a candlelit dinner, or take a sailboat cruise through the bay and out to sea for a spectacular sunset and view of Shirley Heights. The Store also can arrange dive and charter sail packages for the adventurous.

Elsewhere in Antigua

Antigua is one of the larger islands in the West Indies, and elopement options abound. Three highlights follow.

Galley Bay

Galley Bay's thatched-roof Gaugin cottages feature a breezeway and patio that connect each bedroom and boudoir bathroom.

Basic wedding packages include the services of a coordinator and cost $600. For more information, call 800-345-0356 or see www.antigua-resorts.com.

Blue Waters

Blue Waters at Soldier's Bay, remodeled after Hurricane Georges in 1998, offers a wedding package for $550 that features a complimentary honeymoon. Ceremonies here are held in a gazebo at the end of a jetty overlooking the Caribbean. Pre- or postnuptial spa services add to Blue Waters's appeal. For more information, call 800-557-6536, E-mail bluewaters@candw.ag, or visit www.bluewaters.net.

The Admiral's Inn

This is another carefully restored building in the vicinity of Nelson's Dockyard. Room rates include complimentary use of sunfish and snorkeling equipment, as well as transportation to nearby beaches. Call Miss Ethelyn Philip at 268-460-1027 or 268-460-1153, or E-mail admirals@candw.ag for more information.

Nuts and Bolts

Where to Start

Wedding packages at the Copper and Lumber Store cost $350 and include help with the paperwork, the services of a marriage officer, legal fees, a bridal bouquet, breakfast on the morning of the ceremony, a bottle of champagne, and an afternoon or evening cruise. For more information, contact the Copper and Lumber Store directly at 268-460-1058.

Travel Information

Air Canada, American Airlines, and Continental service V.C. Bird International Airport on the northeast corner of Antigua.

Legal Requirements

If you're at least eighteen and getting married for the first time, all you need to be married in Antigua is a passport as proof of citizenship. You must visit the Ministry of Justice on Nevis Street in downtown St. John's to complete an application for a special marriage license and pay the appropriate fees ($150 for the license and $50 for the marriage officer). The ministry is open Monday through Thursday from 8:30 A.M. to 4:30 P.M. and Friday from 8 A.M. to 3 P.M. An additional registration fee of $40 needs to be paid at the courthouse at the corner of High and Temple streets.

Antigua requires that at least two witnesses attend the ceremony apart from the marriage officer. Rounding up spectators at a hotel ceremony never is a problem.

Lead Time

Antigua has no residency requirement, but you'll have to allow time to visit the Ministry of Justice to complete your paperwork. The Copper and Lumber Store requests at least three days advance notice if you require assistance with the paperwork.

When to Go

Antigua enjoys relatively dry and mild weather year-round. What rain does fall (forty-five inches annually) usually is concentrated around September through November. The low season, mid-April to mid-December, features the best deals and fewest crowds, though some hotels and restaurants shutter their doors altogether until the snowbirds arrive around Christmas. The largest of the Leeward Islands, Antigua falls within the hurricane belt from July to November.

Additional Contact Information

The Antigua and Barbuda Department of Tourism phone number is 888-268-4227; you can E-mail info@antigua-barbuda.org, or visit their website at www.antigua-barbuda.org.

Saint Lucia

Cost: $$

Degree of difficulty: Moderate

This West Indian member of the British Commonwealth legitimately and proudly wears its preservation ethic on its sleeve. Saint Lucia was the first local nation to establish a Nature Heritage tourism program to promote sustainable development in the Caribbean. If you're looking for high-rise hotels, casinos, and souvenir shops, elope elsewhere. Instead, the locals here point proudly at institutions such as the Saint Lucia National Trust, established in 1975 through a parliamentary act to promote preservation policies; the Forest and Lands Department, which manages the nineteen-thousand-acre National Rain Forest Reserve; and the Naturalist Society, an educational branch of the Forest and Lands Department.

Saint Lucia has even taken measures to reverse the environmentally devastating effects of sugarcane, which once was the island's principal commercial crop. Today, banana farming, limited timber harvests, and environmentally sensitive exotic flower and orchid growing keep the local economy afloat. That and tourism—Saint Lucia is not just conscientiously green, but literally so. Though the beaches are closed to spear fishing and coral collecting, the lounging is first-rate.

Saint Lucia is the greenest Caribbean nation, literally and politically. (Steve Lucas)

Stonefield Estate, near Soufrière, offers the best of both worlds—leisure without guilt. Stonefield's architects used traditional West Indian methods to build a property that blends gracefully with the local environment. This is one of several small inns on the island that participates in the Nature Heritage program.

The name Stonefield can be misleading, for the twenty-six-acre property rests about one kilometer from sea level—elevated enough for rain forest breezes to descend on the property and support the ferns, bamboos, and flame trees that thrive in a cool environment, but close enough to the Caribbean for bougainvillea to climb walls freely under the sun. Couples utter their wedding vows not far from where a pre-Columbian artist engraved an ancient petroglyph in the shape of a couple and small child—perhaps a symbol for love and hope.

Each of Stonefield's larger villas sleeps five or six guests, but couples will want the smaller, more secluded villas overlooking the sea. A welcoming hammock hangs in a spacious veranda. An intimate outdoor shower also takes advantage of the view.

Unlike other Caribbean islands, Saint Lucia doesn't have to import all of its produce, and you'll taste the advantage of this on your plate at Stonefield Estate. Creamy pumpkin soup, plantain casserole, and fresh-caught kingfish in an aromatic, spicy sauce are typical fare at a restaurant on the property. Or Stonefield can supply your villa with groceries from the local markets in Soufrière—a worthwhile service for an extended stay, given the estate's remote location. The heavenly jug of rum punch in your refrigerator when you arrive is complimentary.

Appetites are earned via hiking in Saint Lucia's intact rain forest, snorkeling, diving, horseback riding, or just lounging on nearby Malgretoute Beach (French for "in spite of it all").

Elsewhere on Saint Lucia

Ladera Resort

Ladera perches eleven hundred feet above sea level between two volcanoes, known as the Pitons. Though completely private, the open-air master bedroom in each suite lacks a fourth wall and enjoys a breathtaking view. For more information, including wedding packages, call 800-738-4752 or see www.ladera-resort.com.

Anse Chastanet

This is Saint Lucia's most remote resort, but worth the ride. Deluxe, open-air suites, located a healthy distance uphill on the property, share their environs with hummingbirds among the treetops. Each room exhibits paintings from artists the property commissions each year. For information about weddings at Anse Chastanet, contact the wedding coordinator directly at 758-459-7000. For general hotel information, call 800-223-1108 or see www.ansechastanet.com.

Saint Lucia's most remote resort, Anse Chastanet, is worth the ride.
(Courtesy of Anse Chastanet)

Pigeon Island

This forty-acre islet is located by the northern tip of Saint Lucia. Historical ruins, manicured lawns, and centuries-old trees make this national landmark a unique and private setting for weddings. Call 758-450-0603 for more information.

Mamiku Gardens

A historical and botanical garden located in southeastern Saint Lucia, Mamiku offers the services of two wedding coordinators. The garden, under the ownership of the Shingleton-Smith family since 1906, is part of a working banana and flower plantation and is a historic spot. Here stand the ruins of Baroness de Micoud's eighteenth-century sugar plantation, where one of the bloodiest slave rebellions in the island's history—known as Brigand's War—was fought. Be sure and visit Mamiku for its fascinating history even if you choose to elope elsewhere. For more information, call 758-452-9176 or see www.mamiku.com.

Nuts and Bolts

Where to Start

Basic wedding packages at Stonefield Estate cost $989 during the high season ($830 during the low season) and include a marriage license and certificate, registrar fees, decorations, a cake, a bouquet for the bride, champagne, a Creole candlelit dinner, and two massages. For more information, call 758-459-7037 or 758-459-5648, or see www.stonefieldvillas.com.

Travel Information

Numerous U.S., European, and Caribbean airlines service Hewanorra International Airport on Saint Lucia on a daily basis.

Legal Requirements

Eloping couples should opt for any of the Saint Lucian hotels, such as Stonefield Estate, that offer wedding packages with the services of a coordinator who will assist with the legal requirements. To marry in Saint Lucia, you must first apply for a marriage license from the attorney general through a local lawyer. You'll also need your passports and birth certificates.

Lead Time

The attorney general requires that applications for marriage licenses be received at least three working days before your ceremony, which jibes nicely with Saint Lucia's three-day residency requirement. Stonefield Estate can arrange a wedding within this time frame as well.

When to Go

The low season (May through October) offers better accommodation rates and availability, but hurricanes or tropical storms may alter your travel plans. Plan ahead if you wish to visit Saint Lucia during the more popular high season (November through April).

Additional Contact Information

For more information, contact the Saint Lucia Tourist Board at 888-4-STLUCIA (888-478-5824). Their website is www.stlucia.org.

Part III

The United States and Canada

There are plenty of exotic elopement sites beyond Vegas and still Stateside, that don't require thirteen-hour flights, inoculations, and the like. North America is convenient that way.

We eloped to Lake Tahoe—it took less than a day, but we stretched the experience over thirty-six hours to get in some prime skiing. Eight additional U.S. and Canadian options are depicted here.

Nevada

Cost: $

Degree of difficulty: No sweat

If there's a better metaphor for marriage than skiing, we have yet to discover it. The thrill that results from flirting with the edge of control—of plunging—is what causes otherwise rational people to wrap themselves in layers of Gore-Tex and goose down and trundle up a mountain in the middle of winter . . . to be married.

The Sierra Nevada mountains surrounding Lake Tahoe are top-notch eloping terrain on several fronts. The far eastern edge of the range spills into the state of Nevada, where the marriage laws are famously elopement-friendly. And the landscape is gorgeous. In sharp contrast to the schmaltzy wedding chapels that populate Las Vegas or Reno further inland, the Sierras are one of Mother Nature's greatest natural cathedrals.

In lieu of neon, wintertime weddings at Diamond Peak Ski Resort in Incline Village, Nevada, are illuminated by bright sun, dry snow, and the glare off indigo-blue Lake Tahoe, which lies at the resort's feet. On the day of our visit, a high-pressure system had flooded the basin with sunshine in the wake of a humongous dumping of snow. It was a Monday, and hundreds of skiers and snowboarders had ditched work and were frolicking in the fresh powder.

The marriage license office following a major dumping of snow

We were met at the base lodge by Diamond Peak sales manager Kurt Althof, who was on hand to assist with the logistics and photography, and by Jay Pearson, a nondenominational minister whose antiestablishment views (broadcast on cable-access television) placed him distinctly outside the local religious community looking in. Our experience is that free spirits make ideal officiants, and Pearson was game to say the least. "What a day," he said, extending his right hand upon his arrival at the lodge. "I hope you don't mind that I brought my skis!"

Pearson had dressed for the occasion in a black ski suit, unzipped a few inches at the neck to expose a white turtleneck—perfect. We changed in Kurt's office into our own wedding clothes (a suit and gown), and added down jackets to buffer us from the crisp air. Though the sun was strong, the thermometer on the outer wall of the base lodge was pinned squarely at thirty degrees. We affixed lift tickets to our jackets, clamped on our skis and snowboard, and headed straight to the front of the lift line. Going first is one of the perks of getting married on a mountain.

Our minister showed up in a black ski suit and white turtleneck—perfect.

Weddings at Diamond Peak Resort are held on a landing connected to a snack shop midway up the mountain. Following our dismount at the top of the chairlift, our first task was to pick a place on the landing for our ceremony that allowed Kurt to capture Lake Tahoe in the background in all its splendor, yet avoid the lens-shattering glare of the midday sun. Once we'd settled on the proper perspective, we moved some picnic tables around the deck to clear space.

A handful of curious sunbather/skiers outside the snack shop put down their hot chocolates to witness our vows. Others did not—apparently, the sight of a young couple in their wedding finery anywhere in Nevada is no big deal.

Pearson stepped forward and opened a Bible. "Marriage often is described as the convergence of two rivers into one," he said.

"Lake Tahoe is fed by many different streams coming from Nevada, and several streams coming from California, to make up one body of water!" It was possible to chuckle at his exuberance and feel the sentiment of the moment at the same time.

The exchange of rings was enlivened by the potential for catastrophe—a fumbled band might have plunged through the deck into roughly six feet of snow. We placed them cautiously on each other's fingers without incident. The rings slipped on easily in the cold. Pearson pronounced us husband and wife, and invited us to kiss. The resultant applause was muffled by the fact that most of our impromptu audience was wearing ski gloves.

Kurt broke out a sheet cake and several plates from the snack bar, and everyone on the deck enjoyed a slice. Jay, Kurt, and a second witness signed our marriage certificate, which we'd procured

The view from the altar, aka Diamond Peak Ski Resort's snack shop

the day before at a government office at the base of the mountain established expressly for that purpose—emphasis on express. Obtaining the license had occupied ten minutes start to finish, and only because we prolonged the process with a bunch of journalistic questions.

The paperwork done and cake consumed, we bid our tiny wedding party farewell and set off on our own to ski. The Lake Tahoe region comprises the largest concentration of downhill ski areas in the country, seventeen in all, ranging in scale from cozy to world class. Diamond Peak falls somewhere in between, with the attitude/ambiance of a small resort and sufficient height (1,840 feet) to reduce the thickest calves to quivering gelatin by the end of a powder-saturated day. Thin air—the Lake Tahoe region stands at between six thousand and eight thousand feet—adds to the effect. In addition to the priceless view of the lake, Diamond Peak's 655 acres of terrain are pleasantly sheltered. When other mountains in the area are getting pelted with inclement weather, it's possible for the microclimate here (nicknamed "the banana belt") to still yield a stellar day of skiing.

More than a thousand condominium units and vacation home rentals are available at Incline Village, at the base of Diamond Peak. For more information, call the Incline Village/Crystal Bay Visitors Bureau at 800-468-2463 or see www.gotahoe.com.

For city slickers such as ourselves who don't ski more than a handful of times each winter, the first run of the year often starts with a moment of trepidation. Inevitably, however, dormant muscles awake and confidence returns. Halfway down our maiden run, we clicked. Carving coordinated corkscrews, we concentrated contentedly on our own distinct activities yet were aware of each other's presence. We were in sync. Again, if there's a better metaphor for marriage than skiing, we have yet to discover it.

Squaw Creek

The night before our nuptials was spent at the Resort at Squaw Creek in California, half an hour west of Incline Village along the north shore of Lake Tahoe. Squaw Creek, which connects with the Squaw Valley USA ski resort via chairlift, is the fanciest hotel in the region, featuring a cluster of upscale restaurants on the premises within stumbling distance of the rooms—recalibrating your alcohol intake at high altitude takes practice. We chose Italian in the name of romance and stockpiling carbohydrates for the day ahead.

Among Squaw Creek's amenities are a fitness center and spa, a shopping promenade, a cross-country ski cen-

Squaw Creek's ultramodern accommodations are a few pole pushes from the nearest chairlift. (Courtesy of Squaw Creek)

ter (with eighteen kilometers of groomed trails), and a heated outdoor pool. The sight of guests traversing the snowy grounds in their bathing suits was jarring at first, but after a plunge of our own, all was explained. Summers, a Robert Trent Jones, Jr.–designed golf course on the property, is a major draw.

At 403 rooms, Squaw Creek is far from intimate. But if it's variety and luxury you're after, this is the place. Accommodations start at $300 a night during ski season for a forest view, though it's worth chipping in a few extra dollars for a room facing the valley. For more information, call 800-327-3353 or visit the website at www.squawcreek.com.

Elsewhere in Nevada

Huge stretches of Lake Tahoe's shoreline are virtually untouched by human hands—a true wilderness. Elsewhere (read, Nevada) are garish casinos replete with billboards advertising wedding services. Most couples in search of a place to elope will be looking for something in the middle. As Tahoe roadside wedding chapels go, here are two of the more tasteful.

The Lakefront Wedding Chapel

On the California side of the border, this tastefully appointed chapel perches picturesquely on the water's edge with the Sierras as a backdrop. For more information, call 888-WED-TAHOE (888-933-8246) or see www.lakefrontwedding.com.

The Dream-Maker

This facility, located on Lake Tahoe's north shore in Nevada, is surrounded by a pleasant garden and towering pines. The staff also assist couples with the logistics of their big day and can handle just about anything. The company's star-studded roster of clients—The Dream-Maker arranged a quiet ceremony for Tom Selleck—attests to its taste level. For more information, call 800-252-3732.

Nuts and Bolts

Where to Start

Diamond Peak's wedding package is $300 inclusive of transportation to and from the site of the ceremony (via chairlift) and a full day of skiing. For more information, contact Diamond Peak Ski Resort at 775-832-1177 or see www.diamondpeak.com. Pastor Jay Pearson's services are an additional $175. Jay is a thoroughly flexible guy; if you wish to range farther afield than Diamond Peak, contact him directly at 888-871-3161.

Travel Information

Reno/Tahoe International Airport is forty-five minutes from Diamond Peak by car. From San Francisco, the drive is three hours, including a climb up and over infamous Donner Pass, where an expedition of California-bound migrants got stuck in the winter of 1846–1847 and resorted to cannibalism to survive. Carry chains—or get your hands on a four-wheel-drive vehicle—lest ye suffer a similar fate.

Legal Requirements

Such a snap here. Bring your driver's licenses and $35 to the local Washoe County Marriage License Office at 865 Tahoe Boulevard (right at the base of the mountain). You'll walk out minutes later with your marriage license in hand—no muss, no fuss. Note that to accommodate peak ski traffic, the marriage license office is open Wednesday through Sunday, 9 A.M. to 6 P.M., but closes Monday and Tuesday. Also remember that Nevada requires one witness to your wedding. For more information, call 775-832-4166.

Lead Time

There is no waiting period per Nevada state marriage law. The principals in the matter—minister, hotel staff—generally can work their magic with about forty-eight hours advance notice.

When to Go

Outdoor weddings are held at Diamond Peak only during the ski season, which usually stretches from December to April. Weekends are exponentially more crowded than weekdays throughout the Lake Tahoe basin.

Additional Contact Information

For centralized North Lake Tahoe lodging information and reservations, contact the North Lake Tahoe Resort Association at 888-358-7461 or see www.tahoefun.org. The North Lake Tahoe Wedding and Honeymoon Association phone number is 800-358-LOVE (800-358-5683).

Recommended Reading

A significant chunk of the two-and-a-half-inch-thick guidebook *Tahoe: The Complete Guide* from Foghorn Press is devoted to wedding information. Author Ken Castle knows Tahoe to the bone: he once explored the 1,645-foot-deep lake via submarine.

Hawaii

There is no one Hawaii. The Aloha State comprises
more than one hundred volcanic islands and atolls
sprawled across sixteen hundred square miles of the
Pacific Ocean. Six major islands—the Big Island, Kauai,
Lanai, Maui, Molokai, and Oahu—contain the majority of the local population and absorb all the tourist
traffic. Though the islands share similar topographies,
each is distinct from its neighbor in terms of density of
development.

Likewise, to include just one Hawaii chapter in a
book about eloping would be an injustice. Hawaii is the
No. 1 wedding destination in the United States, and
there are hundreds of eloping options contained within.
Here are three.

The Big Island

Cost: $$$$

Degree of difficulty: No sweat

Hawaii's Big Island is, ironically, one of its most tranquil. Since the arrival of Europeans in the nineteenth century, much of the action has shifted to Oahu and the capital of Honolulu. As a consequence, the Big Island houses some of the most secluded locales in the entire archipelago.

Weddings at the Four Seasons Hualalai exploit this sense of serenity to the max. Hualalai feels more like a coastal retreat than a full-blown resort. Of course there's golf here (the resort course was designed by Jack Nicklaus), as well as umbrella-adorned cocktails and sumptuous massages (try the hour-long lomi lomi). But instead of a hivelike hotel, guests room in unobtrusive coastal bungalows bedecked with Hawaiian art and tasteful mahogany and wicker furniture. Private gardens and *lanai* (verandas), meandering stone paths and wooden bridges, and a landscape of tropical foliage and natural lava-rock ponds add to the peaceful vibe.

Weddings here reflect the surrounding sense of calm. Most couples exchange their vows barefoot on the beach, surrounded by a smattering of sunbathers, or alone altogether with their thoughts (and officiant and witness, of course). Another option, The Wedding at King's Pond, is one tick up the activity scale.

At the Four Seasons Hualalai, weddings are held on a platform in the middle of this 2.5-million-gallon outdoor aquarium. (Peter French)

Inspired by natural anchialine ponds found along Hawaii's coasts, King's Pond is a 2.5-million-gallon lava-rock aquarium stocked with more than thirty-five hundred tropical fish, including yellow tangs and unicorn fish. Guests actually snorkel and scuba in the pond, which features a wooden platform floating in the center— a perfect spot for the groom to await the arrival of his bride.

The best time for a King's Pond wedding is late afternoon, just before the Big Island blue sky begins its metamorphosis into a sunset. While the groom heads to the King's Pond platform to sweat out his wait, the bride is escorted through the gardens for photographs. As the sky pinkens, a trio of musicians serenades the guests with melifluous island music. When at last the bride appears, her path to the edge of King's Pond is lit with bamboo torches. A *pu* (conch shell) is blown three times, marking the official beginning of the wedding.

Getting to the platform requires a short canoe trip—propulsion is provided by two pole-wielding escorts. Just as the canoe pushes away from shore, the island music is replaced by Hawaiian wedding chants called *oli*. Once the bride has disembarked, the canoe returns to shore, leaving only the bride, the groom, and the officiant on the platform.

Four Seasons Hualalai weddings are high on symbolism but remain typically (and tropically) lighthearted affairs. The officiant first pours from one blessed bowl to another—a symbol of two lives becoming one. Then the couple's hands are wrapped with maile, a fragrant Hawaiian vine, symbolizing the permanence of their bond. After the pronouncement of marriage, music plays again, and the couple enjoy their first dance, in the middle of King's Pond, as husband and wife.

Nuts and Bolts

Where to Start

A Wedding on King's Pond costs $3,000, which includes the photographer and an album with twenty-four photos; the officiant; musicians; escorts; champagne; flowers; and of course the services of a canoe and paddler, a torch lighter, and a conch shell blower.

Accommodations are extra. Ocean-view rooms at the Four Seasons Hualalai start at $550 per night, though couples who opt for the King's Pond wedding receive a 20 percent discount on the cost of these rooms. The Four Seasons also has special honeymoon packages that can help whittle away the cost of a stay. For more information, contact the Four Seasons Hualalai at 808-325-8000.

Travel Information

Kona International Airport is a mere six miles and two left turns from the Four Seasons on Highway 19. United's morning flights from San Francisco and Los Angeles are the only direct routes between the United States and Kona. Otherwise you're facing a connection in Honolulu.

Legal Requirements

The Four Seasons will make an appointment to procure your marriage license at a neighboring hotel. You'll need to bring a photo ID and, if you've been married before, divorce documentation. The whole process takes about twenty minutes. There is no waiting period. The cost is $50.

Lead Time

Generally speaking, the only hurdle to eloping at the Four Seasons Hualalai is securing a room in advance. Between November and March, when snowbirds flee the wintry mainland en masse in search of sun, reservations can be especially hard to get.

If your ceremony involves just the two of you, the staff wedding coordinator usually can arrange at least a simple ceremony within a week. If a Wedding on King's Pond is more your taste, she'll need a little more notice.

When to Go

The weather is consistently hot and beautiful all year, rendering seasonal considerations moot.

Additional Contact Information

For visitors guides and the like, contact the Kona Visitors Bureau at 808-886-1655 or the Hilo Visitors Bureau at 808-961-5797.

Maui

Cost: $$$$

Degree of difficulty: No sweat

Consider the parallels between golf and marriage. In both disciplines, players ponder their strategies, make careful choices before starting out, and attempt to steer clear of hazards that line their paths. Both entail exhilarating moments and abjectly frustrating ones. With a little practice and proper instruction, participants can improve throughout their lives.

Some of the world's best golf courses undulate through the Hawaiian Islands. The combination of verdant, unorthodox terrain and perfect weather have attracted a cadre of top-shelf course designers including Jack Nicklaus, Arnold Palmer, and Robert Trent Jones, Sr. There are nearly one hundred courses in Hawaii all told.

The Kapalua Resort on Maui consistently ranks at or near the top of the heap. Kapalua is a 1,650-acre community that comprises three golf courses. The Plantation Course weaves through an old pineapple estate and is renowned for its blind shots and perilous changes in elevation. The Village Course forges inland toward the West Maui Mountains. Kapalua's original track, the Arnold Palmer–designed Bay Course, noodles near the sea on high cliffs and has smashing views of Molokai. It's on this course that the Ritz-Carlton Kapalua's golf wedding takes place.

Weddings are no place for golf puns: the Ritz-Carleton Kapalua's Weddings on the Green. (Courtesy of the Ritz-Carleton Kapalua)

The Ritz-Carlton Kapalua's Tee for Two package was created for guests who love golf—a lot. In-house wedding coordinator Adele Grover sums up the three-day package thusly: "It's all golf, all the time . . . with a great massage thrown in, too."

On the day of the ceremony, participants are escorted to a golf cart that's been decorated with orchids and tropical flowers for a ride to the Bay Course's fifth hole. The view is stunning—the tee box sits on the edge of a cliff and looks across the Pacific to Lava Point and Molokai, which still does not contain a single traffic light.

Accompanied by acoustic guitar, the couple walk to the center of a circle of tropical flowers at the cliff's edge. After the ceremony, there is champagne and cake right there on the green and (what else) golf. Couples play the fifth ceremoniously, and trust that the result is not an omen. The tee shot sails directly over Oneloa Bay, and many a ball has been irretrievably lost here.

Nuts and Bolts

Where to Start

The Ritz-Carlton Kapalua's Tee for Two: A Wedding on the Green package costs $5,500 and includes three nights accommodation, two days of golf, massages for two, the ceremony, a photographer, a guitarist, flowers, the cake, and dinner. Options like a horse-drawn carriage or a videographer are extra. For more details, contact the Ritz-Carlton Kapalua at 808-669-6200 or see www.ritzcarlton.com/location/NorthAmerica/Kapalua/main.htm.

Travel Information

There are three airports in Maui. The largest and busiest is Kahului, about a forty-five-minute drive from the Ritz-Carlton. United, Hawaiian Airlines, and American offer nonstop service from Los Angeles to Kahului, which is also serviced by Delta and Northwest.

The Kapalua–West Maui Airport is just five minutes from the resort. Aloha Island Air and Trans Air fly here.

Finally, Hana Airport is a one-strip, one-room operation in the northeast corner of the island. There is one car rental agency, but not much else. Air Molokai and Aloha Island Air use this airport. Note that weekend fares are generally higher in price.

Legal Requirements

Obtaining a marriage license in Maui requires a visit to the home of a licensed agent about five minutes from the resort. The Ritz-Carlton Kapalua sends all the paperwork to guests to complete beforehand, and it's simply a matter of showing up with a driver's license or passport and signing. The cost of the license ($50) is included in the wedding package.

Lead Time

Ritz-Carlton Kapalua wedding coordinator Adele Grover can organize a Tee for Two wedding ceremony with as little as twenty-four hours advance notice.

When to Go

The rainy season is from December to February. Though this usually entails nothing more than brief afternoon showers, the squalls still can dampen a tuxedo in a jiffy. The Ritz-Carlton has a sheltered area for rainy day vows.

February to May is whale season, and sightings of humpbacks off the coast are common. One lucky couple even has a wedding photo of a humpback breaching in the background during their ceremony.

Additional Contact Information

For visitor guides and the like contact the Maui Visitors Bureau at 808-244-3530.

Kauai

Cost: $$$

Degree of difficulty: Doable

Kauai is Hawaii's most rugged island, an assemblage of spectacular cliffs and canyons that is impossible to circumnavigate by car. On the east shore, high mountains jut into the clouds and water flows unceasingly—Kauai also is the only island in Hawaii that has rivers. To the west are endlessly rolling coffee plantations, a dark blanket of green speckled with white flowers or red berries. A lack of infrastructure adds to the island's rustic charm and logistical difficulty. Travelers to Kauai only get half the experience if they stick to terrestrial modes of transportation.

Via helicopter, on the other hand, guests get a bird's-eye view of the inaccessible environs of Kauai. Eloping couples get the view plus a bonus—access to a private waterfall that's an ideal spot for staging a wedding ceremony, followed by a dip in the emerald pool into which it pours. Inter-Island Helicopters, in conjunction with Coconut Coast Weddings, organizes weddings in the wilderness adjacent to spectacular Puu Ka Ele waterfall. The ceremony is for couples who are decidedly *not* afraid of heights: Inter-Island pilots like to fly with the doors off. As pilot Ed Wagner describes it, "The seat ends and there's the earth." Kindly enough, Wagner will put his doors on for poofy wedding dresses.

Coconut Coast's Waterfall Weddings begin at the hangar of Port Allen Airport, where a coordinator and officiant meet guests and escort them to the chopper. After a briefing and instructions on how to use the two-way radio headsets, it's time for liftoff. Helicopters can get into Kauai's nooks and crannies like nothing else—you actually fly into Waialeale Crater, reported to be the wettest place on earth because of its tendency to trap clouds that roll in on the trade winds. The tour also includes a plunge through Waimea Canyon, sometimes described as a miniature Grand Canyon only greener. Should a mountain goat or hidden waterfall catch your eye, Inter-Island Helicopters' pilots are adept at swooping in for a closer look.

After a forty-five-minute flight, the helicopter lights on a helipad near Puu Ka Ele, a hundred-foot spill that tumbles past ferns, trees, and slick rock into an emerald pool. Be sure and bring a bathing suit; no waterfall wedding would be complete without a literal plunge to punctuate the metaphorical one.

Waterfall Wedding ceremonies are accompanied by a chorus of rushing water and usually wrap up in time for a late lunch. Coconut Coast does a gourmet picnic complete with champagne, tiki torches, and linen. Menu items may include cilantro Creole potato salad, poppyseed cole slaw, or grilled veggies with goat cheese. The homemade macadamia nut brownies should not be missed. But don't forget, it's a stomach-churning ride home, too.

Waimea Plantation Cottages, on the sunset side of the island, are restored bungalows dating from the 1840s. They are more cozy than luxurious, but still make for a fine escape. Prices for a one-bedroom cottage start at $215. For more information, call Waimea at 800-922-7866.

For all the amenities, there is always the Hyatt Kauai Resort and Spa at 808-742-1234.

Nuts and Bolts

Where to Start

Although they are separate operations, Inter-Island Helicopters and Coconut Coast Weddings work together to coordinate Waterfall Weddings. Call Coconut Coast first at 800-585-5595. If Coconut Coast is booked, help with the details can be provided by either Bali Hai Weddings at 808-821-2269 or Mohala Wedding Services at 808-742-8777. Inter-Island can be reached directly at 808-335-5009.

The price for the complete two-hour tour and ceremony varies from operator to operator. Coconut Coast charges $2,000, including help procuring a marriage license and the services of an officiant (nondenominational minister John Young). The gourmet picnic is an additional $75.

Travel Information

Hawaiian Airlines and Aloha Airlines both offer regular service to Kauai's Lihue Airport from Honolulu. The Waterfall Weddings tour begins from Port Allen Airport nearby in Hanapepe on the southwest side of the island.

Legal Requirements

Coconut Coast will arrange an appointment to procure your marriage license. All you need to bring is an ID and $50.

Lead Time

Inter-Island Helicopters is the only operator with access to Puu Ka Ele. If there's a booking available, you're in. The more notice you can provide, of course, the better your chances of procuring a reservation, especially for weekend weddings.

When to Go

July and August are the warmest and driest months in Kauai. January and February can be blustery for flying, but still are entirely in play.

Additional Contact Information

For visitor guides and the like, contact the Kauai Visitors Bureau at 800-262-1400.

Wyoming

Cost: $

Degree of difficulty: Doable

Jackson Hole, Wyoming, is an ideal staging ground from which to access some of the greatest wildernesses this continent has to offer. The Grand Teton National Park and much of the Bridger-Teton National Forest fall within Jackson Hole's six-hundred-square-mile natural perimeter. Yellowstone's southern entrance is near enough to share a mailbox.

Though growing, the town of Jackson itself still offers a relatively down-home alternative to the high-altitude glitz that has consumed other mountain communities (let's not name names, but we're thinking of a place that rhymes with "snail"). There are boutiques here, but also feed stores and truck stops.

The community is a lively one, populated with a rich pool of musicians, artists, and colorful coots—many of whom came to Jackson en route to somewhere else and have lingered a lifetime. This description applies to Teton Mountain Weddings proprietor Karen Brody as well as anyone. During a 1992 visit to Jackson while on vacation with her sister, Brody had an epiphany: this seemed like an ideal place to start a wedding business. Within two years, she'd quit her job as a regional sales manager for a southern California corporation and returned to Wyoming for good.

In the wintertime, Teton Mountain Weddings can arrange transportation to and from the altar via dog sled.

(Courtesy of Jackson Hole Chamber of Commerce)

Amangani

After two and a quarter centuries of development, the United States has finally made the big time. Hong Kong–based Amanresorts—known throughout the world and especially in Asia for its ultraluxurious hotels—opened its first U.S. facility (Amangani) in Jackson in late 1998. The gesture stamps our continent with the jet set equivalent of the *Good Housekeeping* seal of approval.

The Aman way is to immerse its guests in unimaginable luxury without any of the attendant iciness. As with its international brethren, the Amangani is an architectural wonder—modern as anything in the valley, yet thoroughly warm and organic. The staff here wear slacks and button-down shirts, and the decor leans heavily on exposed redwood, rattan, and hewn sandstone, overlaid with a contemporary economy of line.

Aman in Sanskrit means "place of peace," and *gani* is Shoshone for "home." Each of the Amangani's forty suites has a stone fireplace and a stellar view of the surrounding mountains. A heated outdoor pool on the property is comfortable, even in the middle of winter, and provides a particularly stirring view of the range.

Rooms at the Amangani start at $500. For more information, call 877-734-7333.

Brody is an ordained interfaith minister and performs many Teton Mountain Weddings ceremonies herself. From her home base in Jackson, she is able to access a staggering variety of mountain terrain for clients' outdoor weddings. Some couples have chartered whitewater rafts for a romantic paddle along the Snake River, pausing to conduct their ceremony during lunch on shore. Other transportation options include snowmobiles, llamas, and horseback.

Dogsled ceremonies offer a unique spin on the wilderness wedding experience. Guests are picked up at their hotel the morning of their ceremony and escorted to the trailhead twenty miles outside Jackson. While the teams and tackle are prepared, the participants are swaddled in mighty blankets—unlike cross-country skiing or snowshoeing, dogsledding is a decidedly non-aerobic means of winter travel.

Each sled transports two people plus an experienced guide. Guests may handle the team if they wish, or defer to their guide. Expertise is not a prerequisite.

The twelve-mile ride from the load-in to the ceremony site traverses an iced-over riverbed and a canyon. Snow-laden conifers lean heavily over the trail. Breaks provide views of the spiky Tetons across the plateau. When the dogs are stopped, they tend to howl with excitement. While underway the sled is miraculously silent—all you hear is the patter of the dogs' bootied feet in the snow, and the whoosh of the wooden runners. Elk, deer, and moose are noticeably unperturbed by the sleds' presence.

The ceremony takes place by a cabin that's operated by the Gros Ventre National Forest Service twelve miles deep in the woods. The facility is strictly functional; a bathroom on the premises is for changing into wedding clothes if desired, though fleece is the unofficial uniform of the region. The main attraction here, however, is supplied by Mother Nature. Following the ceremony, while a crew prepares lunch, the bride and groom are escorted to a thermal hot spring adjacent to the cabin for a celebratory soak. Then it's back into the blankets for the ride out.

A sled dog wedding is a full day, at the end of which couples are dropped off at their hotel and collapse in a heap. Celebratory dinners can be arranged, of course, but Brody has learned from experience not to book up that evening too ambitiously.

The Rusty Parrot Lodge in downtown (as it were) Jackson is a four-star hotel with plenty of charm. Overstuffed beds are especially appreciated during the dead of winter—ditto the jacuzzis that stand in some of the rooms. For more information, call 307-733-2000.

Nuts and Bolts

Where to Start

Teton Mountain Weddings packages start at $300 for Brody's help procuring a license, handling the logistics (including hotel accommodations), and performing the ceremony. Sled dog weddings are an additional $500 per couple. For more information, contact Teton Mountain Weddings at 800-842-0391 or see www.jimedia.com/tetonweddings.

Travel Information

Jackson Hole Airport, in Grand Teton National Park eight miles north of town, is serviced by American, Delta, Skywest, United, and United Express.

Legal Requirements

All you need to do to obtain a marriage license is fill out an application and be at least eighteen years old. It's an honor system thing out West; proof of identification is optional. Both parties must obtain their marriage license in person at the county clerk's office, Monday through Friday, 8 A.M. to 5 P.M.

Lead Time
Teton Mountain Weddings can accommodate as little as one week prior notice, availability permitting.

When to Go
For sled dog weddings, the snow is predictably deep during the dead of winter in January and February. Late fall and early spring may be less punishingly cold, but dicier so far as snow cover is concerned. Summers in the Tetons are brief but stellar.

Additional Contact Information
For lodging/recreation information, contact the Jackson Chamber of Commerce at 307-733-3316. Another valuable resource is www.jhlodging.com on the Web.

New Mexico

Cost: $$

Degree of difficulty: Moderate

License plates in New Mexico say "Land of Enchantment," a phrase that was first applied to this expanse of mountain-interrupted desert long before the advent of rampant sloganeering. Before the New Age artisans, healers, and crystal peddlers began moving to trendy Taos and Santa Fe in droves. Even before there was a state called New Mexico. When Spanish conquistadors arrived here in the 1500s, searching in vain for a legendary city made of white gold and sapphires, they were mesmerized by the sight of the Rio Grande swirling through cactus-lined canyons.

New Mexico's mystique is not some remote, ethereal presence. In places like the Sangre de Cristo mountains, as the sunset turns the rock an eerie blood red and a river twists below, the spiritual vibe packs the same punch as a blow to the nose. Pueblo Indians went so far as to build underground kiva homes in those mountains so that they could commune with the spirits of the underworld.

Today, these kiva ruins are preserved at Pecos National Historical Park, a half hour from Santa Fe. Beside them rest the remnants of a more recent structure, a seventeenth-century Spanish mission church. You see where we're going with this?

This old mission in Pecos National Park is a sacred site for weddings.
(Courtesy Pecos National Historic Park)

Wedding coordinator Clarice Coffey first saw the ruins when she moved to Santa Fe in 1989, but it wasn't until six years later that she was able to convince the park's rangers to let her conduct ceremonies there. With its combination of Native American and Spanish religious significance, the site is the wonderland of spiritual Southwest wedding destinations. Coffey's company, Fairytale Weddings, is the only wedding coordinator allowed to hold ceremonies on the spot.

The ruins are a half-hour limo drive from Santa Fe—transportation is provided by Fairytale Weddings. Ditto the flowers and an altar, which are prepared in advance so that the ceremony can begin as soon as the couple arrives. The view from the site takes in a huge slice of the state, yet is completely free of roads, buildings,

Ten Thousand Waves

Just a few miles from the galleries and boutiques of Santa Fe is a bona fide Japanese health spa, Ten Thousand Waves, tucked at the base of the Sangre de Cristo mountains. The spa seems so far removed from the city it might as well be on another planet, though the entire journey from downtown to hot tub takes less than twenty minutes.

Ten Thousand Waves has ten tubs in all, most of which sit on teak or redwood decks overlooking the pinyons and aspen groves. The Waterfall tub has a red rock deck with falls that cascade into a cold pool. At the bottom of the New Kojiro tub is a pebbled floor. All but two of the hot tubs are private. None require clothing.

Inside the Asian adobe building, guests tiptoe from treatment to treatment in Ten Thousand Waves kimonos and sandals. Massages, facials, and herbal wraps can be purchased in any combination, lasting up to a full day.

A stone-lined path through the pinyons leads to eight guest suites called the Houses of the Moon. Each Japanese adobe-style suite has a full kitchen, fireplace, and futon. An overnight stay is really the way to go—guests have unlimited access to the hot tubs. Rooms at Ten Thousand Waves range from $125 to $205.

For day guests, use of the hot tubs costs $13 to $25 per person. Treatments start at $98 for the herbal wrap and mineral rub. For more information, call 505-982-9304.

Ten Thousand Waves is a bona fide Japanese health spa, near the commercial heart of downtown Santa Fe.

(Courtesy of Ten Thousand Waves)

and any other signs of modern society. It's as if participants have been transported to another more aesthetically uncluttered era.

To maximize the sense of calm, many couples choose to conduct their ruins wedding at dusk, when typical New Mexico sunsets turn the sky deep red and light up the canyons. Arrangements can be made for Spanish guitar to provide a little mood music. But rest assured, Mother Nature supplies ample atmosphere for those who choose to go the silent route.

Fairytale Weddings can provide religious officiants of a variety of faiths or design nondenominational ceremonies to fit a couple's backgrounds and beliefs. Many choose to blend local elements with their own imported values. One recent wedding combined elements of Celtic and Native American cultures: the groom wore a kilt, bagpipes were played, and the couple drank from a ceremonial Native American wedding vase after saying their vows.

There is no shortage of gourmet dining options in Santa Fe for a postwedding meal. Alternatively, Fairytale Weddings can arrange a traditional Southwest spread of tamales and red chile enchiladas served right on the spot.

The ruins are Fairytale Weddings' most popular outdoor wedding site. Another option is a hand-sculpted sandstone shrine just outside of Santa Fe. It is a smaller setting, with mountain views and an intricate network of nearby trails. Indoor ceremonies can be held in town at Spanish-style chapels or private homes.

If the impulse to sample the thriving local adventure sports scene should arise, Fairytale Weddings can arrange whitewater rafting trips and tours to nearby Taos or Bandelier, a national park whose canyons dip down to the Rio Grande. Santa Fe itself boasts some of the country's best mountain biking and hiking. Trails run from the edge of town through creeks and into aspen groves and meadows.

The Inn on the Alameda is Coffey's choice for where to stay. The Inn features a classy Southwest decor, complete with all the perks one would expect from a honeymoon suite: plush robes, in-room fireplaces, and breakfast in bed. Located just off Canyon Road, the Inn on the Alameda is a quick walk from Santa Fe's famous galleries and fancy eateries. Suites range from $312 to $342 per night. For more information, call 505-984-2121.

Nuts and Bolts

Where to Start

Fairytale Weddings' ceremony at the kiva ruins site in Pecos National Historical Park costs $1,200 including the officiant, flowers, music, photography, and transportation. For more information, call 505-438-7116, or see www.santafe.org/fairytale/.

Travel Information

You would think a state capital might have an airport that's easily accessed. Not so for Santa Fe. Turbo-prop connections from Albuquerque are costly, and worse, inconsistent.

A better bet is to fly into nearby Albuquerque International Airport and take a $15 to $20 surface shuttle. The airport, seventy miles south of Santa Fe, is serviced by American, America West, Continental, Delta, Frontier, Southwest, TWA, and United.

Legal Requirements

To obtain a marriage license a couple must visit the county clerk's office in Santa Fe between 8 A.M. and 4 P.M., Monday through Friday, with driver's licenses, passports or birth certificates, and $25 cash in hand.

Lead Time

As a courtesy to the park rangers, Fairytale Weddings asks for at least three days notice for ceremonies at the kiva ruins site. Ceremonies at alternative locations can be arranged in as little as twenty-four hours.

When to Go

Any time from early May through late October is ideal. Winter in northern New Mexico is too cold and icy for a comfortable outdoor ceremony.

Additional Contact Information

The Santa Fe Convention and Visitors Bureau has information on accommodations. Call 800-777-2489.

Florida

Cost: $

Degree of difficulty: No sweat

Sanibel and Captiva, twin barrier islands in the Gulf of Mexico off Florida's southwest coast, offer a unique perspective on the world both literally and figuratively. It's quiet here, with nary a skyscraper or nightclub in sight—that there's little to do except skip stones in the placid sea and quietly contemplate the meaning of life is one of the islands' charms. And by virtue of their location, between mainland Florida and Mexico's eastern shore, Sanibel and Captiva offer a perspective on the world that's outside the norm. Here the sun rises over land and sets over water—a rare sight for denizens of the East Coast.

Sunset weddings are especially spectacular here for this reason, but a tad trite, don't you think? Sunrise weddings sacrifice little in terms of aesthetics and have a certain symmetry to boot. Consider the symbolism of greeting a new day with an optimistic vow of undying devotion, some deep eye contact, and a kiss. Now we're talking.

Patricia (Patsy) Slater is a resident expert on the cycles of the sun and every other wedding-related detail within a hundred miles of the Sanibel area. The islands exert an undeniable pull on some people, and Slater is one. She visited Sanibel nearly thirty years ago on her honeymoon and never left. Since then she has helped more than four thousand couples tie the knot on and around Sanibel and Captiva, first as an innkeeper at a local hotel and, more recently, on her own under the auspices of Patricia Slater's Weddings by the Sea.

For sunrise ceremonies, Slater leaves the exact location undecided until the very last moment so as to maximize her chances of picking the perfect beach according to that day's weather. "One minute off, and you could miss it," she says. "It's exactly like a sunset, only in reverse. First you see these oranges and pinks on the water—rays of the sun reflecting off the morning clouds. Then you see the top edge of the sun, a little speck of orange. And then there's this wonderful, magnificent fireball." Slater, who officiates her weddings, has been known to break off a ceremony midsentence to allow the principals to admire the view.

Another thing about morning weddings: they leave the rest of the day free to celebrate. Many couples return to their hotel for a champagne breakfast. Others linger at the beach, perhaps even go for a swim. One couple shook Slater's hand, and declared their intention of spending the rest of the day deep-sea fishing. "Different strokes for different folks," Slater says with a shrug.

Shelling—collecting shells that wash ashore here en masse from deeper waters farther out in the gulf—is a major pastime on Sanibel and Captiva. Though you needn't be a shell expert to recognize flawless specimens virtually anywhere on the islands, the beach just north of Blind Pass on the Sanibel-Captiva Road is considered especially prime. The Captiva Crouch is what the locals call visitors' preferred shelling posture.

Another impossible-to-miss natural resource on Sanibel is the J. N. "Ding" Darling National Wildlife Refuge, named after a

Pulitzer-Prize-winning cartoonist who also was one of the pioneers of the modern conservation movement within Franklin D. Roosevelt's administration. The refuge is home to hundreds of birds, reptiles, amphibians, and mammals. Kayak is the preferred mode of transportation for viewing egrets, roseate spoonbills, herons, and ospreys up close and personal within a maze of mangroves. By virtue of its flat topography, the biking here is also ideal; the island is latticed by twenty-six miles of bike paths.

Brennen's Tarpon Tale Inn in the heart of Sanibel's Old Town district is within walking distance of historic Lighthouse Beach, where you can shell and enjoy a shady stroll under sea grapes and Australian pines. For more information, see www.tarpontale.com or call 888-345-0939.

Cabbage Key Inn, eight miles north of Captiva and accessible only by boat, is one of South Florida's few remaining old-fashioned, secluded inns. Formerly the winter estate of playwright and novelist Grace Houghton Rinehart in the 1930s, this rustic inn rests on top of an Indian shell mound, unencumbered by modern, commercial distractions. The Key inspired Jimmy Buffett's song "Cheeseburger in Paradise." For more information, call 941-283-2278 between 9:30 A.M. and 3:30 P.M. Eastern Standard Time.

Nuts and Bolts

Where to Start

As a longtime resident of this tight-knit community, Patsy Slater has the local wedding services industry wired. Licenses are a snap; the clerks at the nearest office in Fort Myers know her by name. Ditto for flowers, limos, even child care. You need only specify what sort of wedding scenerio you'd like, and trust Slater to execute the details flawlessly. For more information, contact Patricia Slater's Weddings by the Sea at 800-808-2163 (locally at 941-472-8712), or see www.sanibelcaptivaweddings.com.

Travel Information

The closest airport to Sanibel, Southwest Florida International, is forty-five minutes from the islands by car. Nearly all major carriers service Southwest Florida International with daily flights.

Sanibel and Captiva are approached by car via a causeway that links Sanibel to the mainland at Fort Myers. A wisp of a bridge at Blind Pass links Sanibel to Captiva.

Legal Requirements

Marriage licenses are available at the Lee County Administration Building, 2115 Second Street in downtown Fort Myers, Monday through Friday from 7:45 A.M. to 5:00 P.M. The application process takes about half an hour. Licenses are valid immediately after application and for the next sixty days. The cost is $88.50 cash.

Couples must be at least eighteen years of age and must apply for a license together in person. Valid identification such as driver's license or passport is required. For a second marriage, the clerk needs to know when the previous marriage ended. For divorced or widowed parties, certified copies of divorce or death certificates are necessary if the divorce or death took place within the last six months. If your legal name differs from the name on your driver's license, it's wise to bring a birth certificate. For more information, call 941-335-2278.

Lead Time

Couples from out of state needn't worry about a waiting period. Florida residents, however, must wait three days or participate in four hours of premarital counseling.

Patricia Slater's Weddings by the Sea can arrange a no-frills ceremony in a day.

When to Go
Springtime in southern Florida offers the best balance between not entirely scorching weather and not completely jammed tourist pressure. Summers are dramatically more bearable on Sanibel and Captiva than mainland Florida.

Additional Contact Information
For more information about Sanibel and Captiva, contact the chamber of commerce at 941-472-1080 or see www.sanibel -captiva.org. The Lee Island Coast Convention and Visitors Bureau in neighboring Fort Myers can be reached at 800-237- 6444, or see their informative website at www.leeislandcoast.com.

Vermont

Cost: $$

Degree of difficulty: No sweat

During the buildup to the American Revolution in the early 1770s, southern Vermont was a cauldron of anti-British foment. Marsh Tavern, in tiny Manchester, was a hangout for a cadre of farmers-turned-revolutionaries, dubbed the Green Mountain Boys, who met there regularly to swill beer and plan their insurgency. When the tavern's owner, William Marsh, made his loyalist views an issue, the Green Mountain Boys seized his pub.

What a difference a couple centuries make. Marsh Tavern still stands its ground, but it has been incorporated into an upscale resort, The Equinox, that's fond of wearing its British identity on its sleeve. Equinox guests pick and choose from an array of continental pastimes, including shooting, fly-fishing, and Scotch whiskey sampling. The Equinox's official car is a Land Rover. Gleneagles Hotel in Scotland is a sister property.

Couples wishing to elope at The Equinox also face a menu of options. During the summer, a lush garden immediately behind the hotel is a particularly beautiful and convenient site for a ceremony. In the event of foul weather, the front lobby is suitably grand. For couples who wish to go the full Colonial route, horse-drawn carriages are available to and from the hotel's front door.

A tavern on the grounds of The Equinox resort in southern Vermont predates our Constitution. (Courtesy of The Equinox)

Outdoor weddings during the peak of fall foliage season are Vermont's best punch. Though the precise perfect fortnight for viewing fall colors varies from year to year, there's generally no prettier place on the planet mid-September through mid-October.

Outdoor weddings during this time often are held at Equinox Pond, midway up the mountain. The spot provides panoramic views of the valley below and the mountain's own fir-, yellow birch– and red spruce–covered slopes as a backdrop. Reaching Equinox Pond involves a fifteen-minute trail walk; white wedding pumps are probably a bad idea. And you'll likely share your ceremony with fly-fishermen, falconers, and the like. But there's sufficient splendor to go around. As chlorophyll deteriorates in the fall cool, trace colors in each individual leaf enjoy a brief moment in the sun. Maples become orange or red, tamaracks turn to gold, and oaks show maroon and silver. We won't attempt to conjure up adjectives worthy of the spectacle.

Manchester's thirty-five hundred year-round residents include ten justices of the peace who are on call to conduct legally binding weddings on The Equinox's hotel grounds. Couples who wish to incorporate religious elements into their ceremonies may work with the minister at the local (as in next-door) Congregational church, as well as synagogues and other denominations in the Manchester area.

· · · · ·

Political tides have ebbed and flowed in the centuries since southern Vermont first was visited by expatriate farmers from the mother country. But the aesthetic endures. The countryside surrounding The Equinox is still decorated with gobs of Colonial architecture—white clapboard homes, sharp steeples, slat shutters everywhere—in virtually the same pristine condition as when the region marked the western edge of the British Empire two and a half centuries ago. Marsh Tavern itself is a low-ceilinged, exposed-beamed wrinkle in time. The balance of The Equinox's facilities, however, are relatively new. A $13 million renovation in 1992 put the destination on the global luxury resort map.

The Equinox is named for the gentle peak that towers directly over the hotel. Half of its 183 guest rooms face Manchester's central green, a classic Colonial plot of public space surrounded by the local Congregational church, the county courthouse, and shops. The other half of the guest rooms enjoy views of the mountain. In addition to the main hotel, the property also contains a nine-room guest house, the Charles F. Orvis Inn, which originally served as the fly-fishing entrepreneur's nineteenth-century home. Rooms in the inn are heavy on Vermont marble, cherry wood paneling, and other luxuries—and cost roughly three times more than those in the hotel.

An atmosphere of gentility prevails over the property. Men are requested to wear jackets while dining in the Colonnade dining room during the summer. The facility's magnificent vaulted ceilings and expansive bay windows add to the elegant feel. At the more relaxed end of the culinary spectrum is the Dormy Grill (summers only), whose menu is more in the surf-and-turf vein. Marsh Tavern is the spot for an ambience-rich pint of Guinness and pub meal. All menus at the hotel lean heavily on local farm-fresh agricultural products.

The Equinox offers its guests a buffet of activities from which to choose. The Gleneagles Golf Course is a 6,451-yard gem that holds its own against the verdant landscape from which it was carved. Originally designed by U.S. and British Amateur champion Walter Travis in 1927, Gleneagles was renovated by famed architect Rees Jones in 1991 and is known as one of the best tracks in all of New England—and one of the most woman-friendly courses in the country (so says *Golf for Women* magazine). Like the rest of the resort, Gleneagles has a distinctly British air; its smallish greens appear positively minuscule when viewed against the stately forests that frame the scene.

Students at the Land Rover Driving School at The Equinox venture nowhere near Gleneagles's pristine fairways, opting instead for local logging roads and a custom-built obstacle course that's riddled with puddles, ditches, and the like. The school is the British manufacturer's first dedicated off-road driving school in the United States and operates year-round.

Winters, the golf course serves as an ideal locale for cross-country skiing. The local landscape comprises gentle meadows and steeper slopes, with plenty of greenery (they aren't called the Green Mountains for nothing) around to distract the eye from the sport's inherent exertion. Lessons and guided tours are available. A fitness spa on the grounds offers massage, reflexology, hot muslin wraps, and other postski indulgences.

The British School of Falconry at The Equinox offers introductory lessons at $75 a pop. And falconry is not something you want to dive into without a grasp of the basics.

More advanced practitioners can travel to a local hunting preserve to loose their Harris hawks—noted for their amiability around people and acuity in the field—after quail, pheasant, and rabbit in season. It's all very civilized: barbour jackets and boots are provided, and transportation to and from the hunting ground is via Land Rover.

Mount Equinox, the tallest peak in the Taconic Range, avails itself to all-day hikes or hour-long strolls, horseback rides, and mountain-biking. From the thirty-eight-hundred-foot summit, visitors enjoy panoramic views of much of southern Vermont. Trailheads are a short amble from The Equinox's front door.

A fourteen-acre pond on the property scratches the itch for fly fishermen. True diehards will insist on a pilgrimage to the nearby Battenkill, one of the most celebrated stretches of water on the eastern seaboard. Private instruction is available via the hotel concierge, as are extended stays at the Orvis Fly Fishing School. And the American Museum of Fly Fishing is located next door to the hotel.

The Orvis Shooting School and Tinmouth Hunting Preserve offer private upland bird shooting, September through March, and sporting clays year-round.

The Village Shops at The Equinox, located across the village green from the hotel, feature boutique-quality Vermont clothing, crafts, and antiques. Major-league outlet shopping, including Orvis company HQ for fishermen, is within easy striking distance in downtown Manchester. Good old American commerce—there's one Equinox activity our founding fathers would approve of.

Nuts and Bolts

Where to Start

Three-day, two-night Tying the Knot packages start at $1,115 per couple and include arrangements for a justice of the peace, two nights in a suite, breakfasts in bed, dinner each evening, and a bottle of champagne upon arrival. For more information about eloping at The Equinox, contact 800-362-4747 or see www .equinoxresort.com.

Travel Information

The Equinox is located in southern Vermont, a healthy haul (approximately an hour and a half) from the closest major airport in Albany, New York; four hours north of Manhattan; and three hours west of Boston by car. But there are few prettier drives anywhere on the planet, especially during fall foliage season.

Legal Requirements

Vermont nonresidents must purchase their marriage license for $20 in person in the county in which they plan to marry. In Manchester this means a visit to the village town clerk during normal business hours, Monday through Friday. It's within walking distance from The Equinox's front door.

Though technically not required, couples are wise to arrive with their birth certificates in hand. Those who are divorced and widowed also may be asked to provide documentation demonstrating their ability to remarry.

Lead Time

Space permitting, The Equinox can accommodate elopements with as little as twenty-four hours advance notice. However, be sure to arrive in time to procure a license from the town clerk.

When to Go

Though lining up a room and wedding can take some fancy footwork during peak leaf-peeper season mid-September through mid-October, it's worth the effort, as anyone who's ever caught southern Vermont on a pristine fall day can attest. Winters are measurably more low-key and equally romantic. Though weddings are blocked out during holidays, The Equinox is decorated for Christmas the Monday following Thanksgiving through New Year's Day.

Recommended Reading

Anything by Robert Frost, who had the snowy New England winter thing down pat, should put you in the mood.

Additional Contact Information

For more information about visiting Vermont, contact the Vermont Chamber of Commerce at 802-223-3443 or visit www.govtn.com on the Web.

Arizona

Cost: $

Degree of difficulty: Moderate

A prayer is recited during traditional Apache weddings that solicits for married couples enduring companionship, as well as permanent shelter from the rain and the cold. It's a tall order by Euro standards, but within the realm of plausibility among Native American cultures. For centuries Apaches have stressed the tie between spirituality and nature in everyday life. Ceremonies such as weddings are rife with references to this connection.

Arizona is the de facto capital of Native American society nowadays. Nearly one-seventh of all Native Americans in the United States live on reservations that cover a quarter of the state. As a consequence, many Arizonan communities have evolved in harmony with the environment and not at its expense. Buildings emerge from red rock cliffs. Indigenous plants dominate local landscapes. Visitors come to Arizona to see its natural monuments and Indian relics, not shopping malls or amusement parks.

Ditto couples in search of a spot to elope. Some of the most spectacular scenery in Arizona is in and around Sedona. On a clear day, the contrast between the dark pink sandstone and the bright blue sky here is almost blinding. This is the setting in which Weddings in Sedona stages its Red Rock Crossing marriage ceremonies.

The wedding site is a clearing at the end of a quarter-mile trail that can be hiked, even in full wedding garb, without snagging much juniper or gravel. The trail is not quite as secluded as it is beautiful, and curious tourists can turn a private elopement into a wedding procession of more than a dozen impromptu guests. Weddings in Sedona provides a gown-coordinated wildflower bouquet and boutonniere, as well as a photographer. For an additional fee, a flutist will play Native American melodies during the walk.

Red Rock Crossing seems to have been designed by Mother Nature with weddings in mind. It sits between a natural sandstone formation called Cathedral Rock and a pair of buttes known as the Two Lovers. Oak Creek flows nearby, and the sound of rushing water is sufficient background music for most couples.

Weddings in Sedona will provide couples with recreation and accommodation referrals for the days surrounding their ceremony if they wish. A popular prewedding spot is Fango Hair and Day Spa in Sedona, where couples soothe premarital jitters with hot soaks and professional head-to-toe massages. The Himalayan Rejuvenation Treatment is a two-hour process involving a sinus steam, massage, exfoliation, and a "third eye" sesame oil treatment said to eliminate negative energy. Fango is located in a peach-colored, renovated private home with a shaded backyard, in which guests spend hours lounging between soaks and rubs. The spa also offers wedding-day hair and makeup services. For more information, call 520-204-9880.

After the ceremony, newlyweds often retreat to a hillside bed-and-breakfast called the Wishing Well, where three of the five rooms have hot tubs on their private decks overlooking the national forest. The Wishing Well's owner has been known to personally deliver a homemade breakfast of crêpes, berries, and pastries to guests. The Wishing Well even allows small wedding ceremonies by the pond in the backyard.

For those who believe the mind-body connection is exercised through activity, mountain-biking Sedona's famous Bell Rock trail is one day-after option. Lounging in Wishing Well robes by the private fireplace in each guest room can engender a similar state, however. We'll let you guess which is the most popular.

Rooms at the Wishing Well range from $140 to $170. For more information, call 520-282-4914, or see www.sedona wishingwell.com.

Nuts and Bolts

Where to Start

Getting married in a Sedona Red Rock floral wedding at Red Rock Crossing starts at $435, including minister, flowers, thirty-six photographs, a booklet, and a certificate. In addition to the ceremony itself, Weddings in Sedona will help coordinate logistics ranging from lodging and transportation to balloon and jeep tours. For more information, contact Sandy Erzine at 800-9-RED-ROCK (800-973-3762) or by E-mail at romance@sedona.net. The website is www.weddingsinsedona.com.

Travel Information

Phoenix Sky Harbor International Airport, 120 miles south of Sedona, is serviced by Alaska Airlines, America West, American, Continental, Delta, Frontier, Midwest Express, Northwest,

If the Spirit Room Moves You

A different sort of spiritual experience can be sought at the Spirit Room bar in Jerome, a former mining town in the mountains not far from Sedona. The Spirit Room is a regular road stop for some of the Southwest's best reggae, rock, and folk bands. The bar's name is telling, too. "Spirit" refers not only to the liquor and the dancing, but also to the fact that until recently, Jerome was a ghost town.

During the copper boom of the late 1800s, miners and their entourages turned Jerome into one of the West's most populated cities. But they abandoned it when the stock market crashed in 1929. For decades Jerome was reduced to a dusty wasteland of dilapidated bars, jails, and brothels until, little by little, merchants started renovating buildings and opening up copperware shops, inns, and cafés. Jerome is now on the verge of becoming downright cute, but there's just enough ruggedness intact to spare it. The Spirit Room is a case in point. Everything about it—the saloon-style bar, the beer-splotched floor, the denim-clad clientele who view their motorcycles as steeds—oozes Old West. And the music rocks.

The Spirit Room, open from 10 A.M. to 1 A.M., is located at Main Street and Jerome Avenue. For a music schedule, call 520-634-8809.

Southwest, TWA, United, and US Airways. From there, Sedona-Phoenix Shuttle (520-282-2066) offers a round-trip fare of $55.

Legal Requirements

The only trick to getting your marriage license here is finding your way to the county clerk's office in Camp Verde (it's a quick detour en route to Sedona, but only if you're in a rental car). Call 520-567-7741 for directions. The clerk's office is open Monday through Friday, 8 A.M. to 5 P.M.

Otherwise, it's simple—no blood test, no residency requirement, no waiting period. All that's required is a photo ID that proves you're over eighteen.

Lead Time

Arizona is perfect for getting married on a whim. Weddings in Sedona has performed same-day ceremonies in its recent past. But owner Sandy Erzine prefers a couple weeks' warning.

When to Go

The most predictable weather of the year is late spring, when daytime temperatures hover in the upper seventies and rainfall is minimal. Late spring is also when the desert flowers bloom, though you never have to worry about a shortage of brilliant colors on the red rock any time of year.

Early summer brings with it the Southwest's powerful thunderstorms, which generally roll in with a vengeance in the late afternoon and blow away just as quickly—darkening the rock, cleaning the air, and leaving behind a fresh wet scent. If you don't mind getting a little damp, those storms are wonderful mood setters.

Additional Contact Information

Recreation information, including hiking and biking trail guides, can be obtained from Arizona State Parks in Phoenix (602-542-4174).

For additional information on accommodations, call the Sedona Chamber of Commerce at 520-282-7722 or Arizona Tourism at 800-842-8257.

British Columbia

Cost: $

Degree of difficulty: No sweat

If you're a tourist-based business on Vancouver Island, off the coast of mainland British Columbia in the northwest corner of the North American continent, you'd better figure out a way to capitalize on the rain. Summer months are predictably sunny and mild here, but they account for just a fraction of every year. The rest of the time is stormy.

November through February is particularly turbulent. During these months low pressure systems roll seamlessly off the Pacific and bump up against the inland Coast Range, depositing their cargo as they climb. The west coast of Vancouver Island averages nearly 120 inches of rain annually. Until recently, foul weather was a marketing hurdle that no vacation destination in the region had attempted to overcome.

Since it opened for business in 1996, however, The Wickaninnish Inn has been turning the local tourist season upside down. Situated on a rocky promontory at the western edge of Chesterman Beach, overlooking the open ocean, "The Wick" was built with foul weather in mind. Overstuffed chairs and down duvets in the guest rooms are for nesting against the raging weather, and cozy fireplaces abound. Every room enjoys a view

The Wickaninnish Inn, aka "The Wick," on a rare sunny day
(Adrian Dorst)

of the surf—many have views from the soaking tubs in the bathrooms.

Weddings are appropriately low-key affairs at The Wick. Weather permitting, Chesterman Beach is a no-brainer choice of venue. A hidden cove on the property, known appropriately enough as Hidden Cove, also is a perennial favorite. One couple went so far as to wear wet suits beneath their wedding clothes for a postceremony frolic in the sea on boogie boards. When the weather drives weddings indoors, guest rooms are as romantic a locale as anyplace else at the inn.

Confirming the developers' collective hunch, The Wickaninnish has become a popular draw during the winter months specifically because of the lousy weather. At the height of a storm, the action can be wildly entertaining. Waves here grow twenty-five feet tall, and have been known to carry entire trees ashore and pitch them at the inn's feet like armfuls of kindling.

When the sun does make its presence felt, local activities abound. Most capitalize on the region's healthy ocean ecosystem, and proximity to Pacific Rim National Park. Tofino, the quiet village (year-round population: twelve hundred) in which The Wickaninnish Inn is located, marks the National Park's northern boundary.

Hiking in the local old-growth forests is a singular pleasure. Here five-hundred-year-old Sitka spruce trees tower three hundred feet or more above their surroundings, and Western hemlock and red cedar grow to similarly neck-snapping heights. Closer to eye level is a verdant soup of moss, shrubs, and ferns, latticed with enormous felled trees that are moldering in their aboveground graves.

A function of its proximity to Clayoquot Sound, Tofino also is a major hotbed for kayaking. And the whale watching here is world class. Between March and May, an estimated twenty thousand gray whales migrate past Tofino en route from Baja to the Bering Sea. When conditions are right (meaning calm), it is possible to spot the massive mammals on the horizon from the inn itself, sans boat.

Sea lions, harbor seals, porpoises, cormorants, loons, puffins, blue herons, and orcas also ply the local ocean and nest among the rocky cliffs. Though the Pacific here is frigid and unfriendly for swimming, the surfing can be prime. Boards and wet suits are available for rent in and around Tofino.

Many guests, however, come to The Wickaninnish solely to huddle against the storms, venturing beyond the reach of their fireplace only to dine at the on-site restaurant or to stroll on

Chesterman's Beach during breaks in the rain. Put it this way: while other hotels supply bath robes, The Wickaninnish Inn places yellow slickers in each room.

Hot Springs Cove

At Hot Springs Cove, approximately thirty miles north of Tofino, near-boiling water bubbles continuously to the surface and pours over a waterfall into a series of pools, providing soothing relief from the bone-chilling, damp winter air. Visitors can tailor their soak experience according to their pain threshold. The first pool is essentially uncooled; the third alternates between comfortable and frigid, depending on the tide. Most people opt for the middle.

Hot Springs Cove is accessed by boat (there are no roads), a voyage of approximately an hour and fifteen minutes each way, followed by a 1.5-kilometer stroll through the rain forest on a cedar boardwalk constructed expressly for the purpose. Expect to pay in the U.S. $70 to $80 range for the day, lunch not included. If that seems steep, keep in mind the possibility of spotting sea lion colonies or orca whales in their natural environment en route. For more information, contact Chinook Charters (800-665-3646) or Jamie's Whaling Station (250-725-3919).

Seaplanes are available, at a price, for those who can't wait to get in the pool. For more information, contact Tofino Airlines (250-725-4454).

Nuts and Bolts

Where to Start

There is no actual wedding package available through The Wickaninnish Inn, though the West Coast Romance Package comes close enough to what an eloping couple would typically wish for. Romance packages range from Can$490 (approximately U.S.$335) during the storm-watching season (November through February) up to Can$730 (U.S.$500) during the summer and include two nights accommodation, breakfast delivered to the room, chocolate-dipped fruit, and sparkling wine. For more information, call 800-333-4604 or see www.wickinn.com.

Travel Information

The lone obstacle to eloping at The Wickaninnish Inn, it seems, is getting there. Tofino is located literally at the end of the road where the Trans-Canadian Highway deadends at the Pacific. Driving from mainland Vancouver requires a ferry ride of nearly two hours as well as some seriously twisty stretches of asphalt.

Flying is an easier option, and on a clear day sacrifices little in terms of scenery. The nearest major airport in Vancouver, British Columbia, is serviced by several major carriers. From there, North Vancouver Air flies puddle jumpers to Tofino at a cost of approximately Can$100 (U.S.$68). Inn accommodations can be booked via the airline, and vice versa. Contact either North Vancouver Air (800-228-6608) or The Wickaninnish Inn (800-333-4604) for details.

Scheduled service is offered from Seattle's Renton Field on a seasonal basis through Sound Flight (800-825-0722). Travel time is approximately fifty minutes from Vancouver International Airport, and one hour and fifteen minutes from Seattle's Renton Field.

Round-trip shuttle service, taxis, and rental cars are available from the Tofino Long Beach Airport by advance arrangement.

Legal Requirements

Marriage licenses are available at the Village Government Office in Tofino, Monday through Friday, during normal business hours. The cost is Can$100 (approximately U.S.$68). At least one of you must appear in person, bearing proof of identification of both of you, to obtain the license. You'll need to scratch up a couple witnesses for the actual ceremony, but this is never a problem. Snap weddings are grand entertainment.

For civil ceremonies, expect to pay an additional U.S.$125 to $150 for the marriage commissioner's (officiant) services.

Lead Time

Though there is no waiting period required by BC law, it's considered polite to give The Wickaninnish three days notice of your intentions so they can help line up an officiant.

When to Go

November through February, the weather on Vancouver Island is at its worst, which means The Wickaninnish is at its coziest. The gray whale migration reaches its peak March through mid-May.

Additional Contact Information

The Tourism Association of Vancouver Island can be reached at 250-754-3500.

Ontario

Cost: $

Degree of difficulty: No sweat

When nine packhorses carried a pair of wealthy newlyweds to Niagara Falls in 1801, a North American nuptial phenomenon was born. Niagara Falls "bridal tours" became all the rage among new couples. Within no time, Niagara had earned a reputation as the Honeymoon Capital of the World.

Why? It's something in the water. These falls do not cascade—they plummet furiously and dramatically in impressive walls of water so white, they have the appearance of snow. It's an evocative sight. Charles Dickens, while crossing the mist-filled Niagara River below, wrote that being next to Niagara Falls was like being "next to his Creator."

These days, tour buses have replaced packhorses as the preferred mode of transportation in these parts. Predictably, with the tourists have come souvenir shops and perfectly placed scenic overlooks fashioned from concrete. At night the falls are illuminated with a rainbow of garish spotlights—a delight for some, unnecessary artifice for others. But in spite of the tourist trappings, the falls remain mesmerizing. If you can handle a bit of kitsch, this is a great place to take the biggest plunge of your lives.

Niagara Falls is not one specific location, but a trio of waterfalls that span the Canada–U.S. border. Two cities on opposite

Weddings and Niagara Falls go together like H_2 and O.
(Marco Formisano)

shores of the Niagara River lay claim to the moniker Niagara
Falls: Niagara Falls, Ontario, and Niagara Falls, New York.
Stateside are the American Falls and the Bridal Veil Falls (a nuptial theme is ever-present). Canada claims Horseshoe Falls, a
spectacular concavity of frothing water some twenty-two hundred
feet wide.

Sadly, the New York side is a little run down these days and
known more for its outlet malls than its heavenly ambience. But
the area surrounding Horseshoe Falls has been picking up steam.
In addition to an impeccably maintained fifty-six-kilometer hike-
and-bike trail, the Ontario side boasts a casino, a butterfly con-
servatory—and expert wedding consultants. Staff coordinators at
Occasions in Niagara share an infectious enthusiasm for their job.

They're also intimately familiar with the Niagara area and quick to offer free advice about activities before and after your wedding. And the kicker: they're honest. Rather than pile on another commission, if a location is busy and full of other brides, Occasions in Niagara will say so.

This last point is no small thing. With more than 20 million visitors annually, Niagara Falls is not an ideal destination for those who wish to exchange vows far from the madding crowds. Couples bedecked in their wedding finery are popular subjects for camera-toting tourists. On the other hand, a rainbow arching above an apparitional cloud of mist makes a pretty spectacular backdrop for a ceremony. Occasions in Niagara doesn't guarantee the rainbow (it does appear over Horseshoe Falls most days), but they do promise you will enjoy a view of all three falls at the Oakes Garden Theater, an amphitheater-style garden of clipped lawns, colonnades, and manicured trees that's available for weddings.

Should you decide a falls view is important enough to brave the throngs, an Occasions at Niagara coordinator will meet you at your hotel and transport you (the limousine is an option) to the garden. There you will be met by a nondenominational officiant, married, and sent on your way.

Occasions in Niagara also has a few other outdoor locations from which to choose—and some indoor ones, in case of an uncooperative squall. A botanical garden is one possibility, though it's also known to be packed with brides on summer Saturdays and has no view of the falls. A more private option is the gazebo at Niagara-on-the-Lake, a small town outside Niagara Falls proper. The roar of the falls may be far in the distance, but then again, so are the people. For inclement weather, a chapel is available. There is no one perfect spot; it really depends on the balance to be struck between your privacy and your view of the falls.

The Niagara Falls Marriott is the hands-down winner in the room-with-a-view category. The hotel is literally a stone's throw from the brink of Horseshoe Falls, and every one of its 285 rooms has a rip-roaring view of the hydraulics. Many rooms also have fireplaces, or Jacuzzis, or both. Romantic stuff.

Rates start at Can$119 (approximately U.S.$80) and range well up into three figures for deluxe accommodations. Note that some of the rooms on the lower floors are actually closer to Horseshoe Falls than those at the top. For more information, contact the Marriott at 905-357-7300.

Niagara by Bike

Wine and romance go together without question. So it seems only natural that the Honeymoon Capital of the World is hard by an extensive wine region. The Niagara escarpment and Lake Ontario combined form a surprisingly grape-friendly microclimate despite the cold—ice wine is a popular local product. And vineyard country is always easy on the eyes.

White wines are especially successful here, including pinot gris, riesling, and chardonnay. Most local wineries (there are approximately forty in all) have tasting rooms where guests can sidle up to the bar and sip the various apellations. Many offer tours of their wine-making facilities and cellars.

A great way to connect the dots is with the help of Steve Bauer Bike Tours Inc., which operates one-day excursions around Niagara's wine country. From the launch spot midmorning, each guest is issued a new Schwinn hybrid bike and helmet. After that, it's an easy pedal to one of the larger wineries for a private wine-making tour. Lunch is a gourmet picnic. Afternoons are spent at the tasting rooms of the smaller wineries.

The pace is slow and easy, but power pedalers can be accommodated. A support van carries the gear and food—and also makes sure guests make it home safely.

Bauer is well qualified to run a biking business. He won a silver medal in the 1984 Olympics and competed in the Tour de France eleven consecutive times. He also has romance in his heart: he and his wife, Annick, married in Costa Rica in a hidden hotel. The tours generally go off in groups, but Bauer is happy to customize his service for fellow romantics in search of a more intimate experience.

One-day group tours run Thursday through Sunday, late May through October. The cost is Can$90 to $100 (approximately U.S.$60 to $70). Custom tours are indi-vidually priced. For more information, call Steve Bauer Bike Tours Inc. at 905-562-0788 or see www.steve bauer.com.

Nuts and Bolts

Where to Start

Occasions in Niagara wedding packages start at Can$295 (approximately U.S.$200) for a chapel ceremony that includes such perks as a wedding welcome package, celebratory champagne, and a dozen roses. The Diamonds and Caviar Package, which also includes a photographer, a stretch limousine, and a cake, is Can$875 (about U.S.$600).

Use of the Oakes Garden Theater is an additional U.S.$50, and the botanical gardens U.S.$100. For more information, contact Occasions in Niagara at 905-357-7756 or see www.occasionsniagara.com.

Travel Information

Buffalo Niagara International Airport, a half hour from the falls, is serviced by American, Continental, Delta, Northwest, United, and US Air. Alternatively, travelers coming in from the western United States may be able to procure better fares by routing the trip through the Pearson International Airport in Toronto, an hour and a half northwest of the falls. Both airports have shuttle services to Niagara Falls.

Legal Requirements

For first-timers, obtaining a marriage license in Niagara Falls is easy as pie. Just show up with identification (original birth certificate, driver's license, or passport) at the Clerk's Department of Niagara Falls City Hall, Monday through Friday, between 9 A.M. and 4 P.M. and fill out an application. The whole thing takes about ten minutes. The cost is Can$75 (about U.S.$50).

If you're divorced, you will need to obtain a legal opinion from an Ontario lawyer—not a difficult process, but one that does take up to six weeks to complete. Occasions in Niagara can recommend a lawyer for you.

Lead Time

The Honeymoon Capital of the World is fast becoming the Marriage Capital of the World, and availability is an issue. If you can elope during the week and are flexible about the exact location of your ceremony, Occasions in Niagara can probably accommodate you with as little as two days' notice.

When to Go

For outdoor weddings, the warmest months are June through September, though May and October are entirely doable. During the winter months, when snow arrives in buckets, the falls take on a special kind of frozen splendor that is certainly worth a cold toe or two. But it would be smartest to stage your ceremony inside next to a cozy fire.

Additional Contact Information

The Niagara Falls Visitor and Convention Bureau can help with accommodation and attraction information. Contact them at 905-356-6061.

Part IV

Weddings at Sea

No, it's not true that any old ship's captain can perform wed-dings at sea—at least not according to United States maritime law. It was something of a shock to us too.

But plenty of countries do recognize captains' rights to per-form affairs of the state at sea. And major cruise companies increasingly are working weddings at sea into their arsenal of indulgences.

What follows is a smattering of options. Aboard a twenty-person yacht in the Galápagos, we came to know our compatri-ots—and a few local sea lions—up close and personal. Huge cruise ships such as those operated by Carnival and Princess cruises are less personal, but more accessible. It's a big world, and most of it's water.

Ecuador

Cost: $$$

Degree of difficulty: Doable

The Galápagos Islands off the coast of Ecuador are where Charles Darwin first gathered the famous finches that eventually formed the basis of his theory of evolution by natural selection. Today, nearly the entire archipelago is preserved as a national park, and is still literally crawling with exotic animals—iguanas that swim in the sea, frigate birds whose chests puff up like crimson balloons—that are unafraid of humans to a degree that mocks our habitual arrogance in these matters. One time our entire tour group, twenty people strong, was halted in its tracks by an obstinate booby bird that was hogging our trail and refused to step aside. Later we were sneezed on by a baby sea lion.

There's nothing romantic about being sneezed on by a sea lion when it happens. But moments such as these add up quickly in the Galápagos and create a curious sensation in the stomach when considered in toto. Soon enough you start to perceive each individual element of the local ecosystem, including yourself, as part of a larger whole. The Galápagos will open your eyes in a hurry to the enormity of the living world, and your own relative insignificance in the face of a force as powerful as natural selection. To elope in

One must be watchful in the Galápagos, so as not to be sneezed on by a sea lion.

the Galápagos is to clutch at something stable in a changeable world.

• • • • •

We were unaware of the degree of natural abundance that awaited us when we arrived at the airport in San Cristóbal, the Galápagos' sleepy capital. As we walked across the tarmac toward the terminal, we spotted our first finch, flitting among some weeds that grew through a crack in the asphalt. More than a few people from our flight stopped to take a picture, the Galápagos equivalent of cleaning out the first souvenir shop in Tijuana.

From the dozen or so tour companies that ply the Galápagos we had chosen to travel with Ecoventura, which is known as one of the cushier outfits. Our first impression of our motor yacht was that it was freshly painted and meticulously clean. The *Eric* (breaking with tradition, Ecoventura's owner had named the ship for his grandson), was built in 1990 specifically for the purpose of transporting tourists from island to island in the Galápagos. It featured accommodations for twenty visitors and ten crew members on two decks, arranged around a comfortably large meeting area and booths for meals. A third deck was open to the air and car-

Our ship, the Eric

peted with AstroTurf—an ideal setting for an onboard wedding, despite the absence of air conditioning.

The *Eric*'s resident naturalist, Ivonne Torres, immediately took charge, summoning us via intercom from our rooms to the meeting area on the middle deck so that she could walk us through some things to know about our boat. "Navy showers" (short and cold) would ensure that our onboard supply of fresh water would last all four days. We should settle our drink tabs at the end of our stay. We would be motoring from destination to destination during our nights, though the captain would wait until the wee hours to fire up the engines so that we could fall asleep first. Days would be spent either exploring the islands or resting aboard ship for our next foray.

Then Ivonne made an announcement that was startling compared with the mundane details that had preceded it. "And we have something veeery special tomorrow," she said, her confident English betraying a hint of an accent. "Lisa and Sam would like you to join them at their wedding ceremony performed by the captain." There was a very pregnant pause, then a collective gasp from our yacht-mates. Then applause. All eyes were upon us. "So you have twenty-four hours to talk us out of it," was all Sam could think to say.

• • • • •

Wrote Darwin, upon disembarking the *Beagle* for the first time in the Galápagos: "The birds are strangers to Man and think him as innocent as their countrymen the huge Tortoises." To this day the animals here hardly flinch at the sight of humans in their realm. At the trailhead before our first hike, Ivonne gathered our group and implored us not to touch the wildlife, an admonition that was made necessary by their amazing patience for humans. "Give them some space, basically," she said. By this she meant one or two feet.

As our eyes adjusted to the surreal environment, we saw that the beach was in fact writhing with life. Finches flitted from branch to branch in the underbrush—not skittish, just active— while sizable pelicans dove for fish in the surf. On the shore were marine iguanas by the dozen, lazing passively among a small army of energetic crabs. One could understand how Darwin made his great mental leap here, or at least took the first step (twenty years elapsed between his visit to the islands and the publication of *The Origin Of Species*). It's hard to stand on a seashore in the Galápagos and *not* notice who's eating whom, what's hiding from what, how it all fits together.

The Galápagos will make your head spin that way. In your face at every turn are examples of natural selection in action . . .

and corresponding questions that seemingly would undermine the process. If every element of the ecosystem is held in check by a predator, why were some beaches crawling with fire-engine red crabs that should be easy pickings? If all animals feel an imperative to reproduce, why do blue-footed booby birds practice fratricide? Though Ivonne's professional training was in tourism, it's impossible to spend seven years aboard a boat in the Galápagos and not absorb some evolutionary biology. She fielded each question confidently.

• • • • •

Our four days in the Galápagos quickly fell into a routine, scripted to maximize the morning cool and avoid the midday heat.

First thing after breakfast we would evacuate the boat for a nature hike on a nearby island. A typical hike lasted approximately two hours, and we never failed to encounter myriad strange animals and plant forms. On Hispaniola Island, it was the Sally lightfoot crabs, whose orange shells are explained by the fact that they face no known predators. On Floreana Island, we visited a lagoon in which a flock of pink flamingos foraged along the perimeter. The trail then worked its way up over the crest of the island—land masses in the Galápagos Islands usually feature a volcanic hump—providing an elevated view. In the water below we could see a marine turtle kicking up a trail of mud. "It's not supposed to be in there," Ivonne said, a shade of concern crossing her face. "If it doesn't find a way out it will probably die." Survival of the fittest indeed.

Afternoons were spent swimming and snorkeling in the sea. The underwater action was spectacular. One time we visited an outcropping of rock via dinghy about half a mile from where the *Eric* was moored. Right off the bat we saw a huge school of silverfish, then a tornado rocketing through our field of vision below—a sea lion. Shouting into a snorkel makes a funny kind of desperate noise. No one can hear you, not even yourself.

Moments before reboarding the dinghy, we drifted over a small galaxy of starfish that stood in precise relief against an expanse of sand on the ocean floor. It was like a miracle, such order amid the chaos. When we finally reboarded the skiff, everyone was chattering. Adrenaline apparently has the same affect on adults as it does on children.

· · · · ·

Our wedding clothes emerged miraculously unruffled from their garment bag; we had feared that the heat and humidity would fold them permanently in half. We weren't exactly nervous, though a jolt of adrenaline shot through our cabin when Ivonne announced over the PA system that our ceremony would begin in half an hour. When we finally emerged, the hallway and stairs outside our cabin had been decorated with makeshift ribbons fashioned from twisted toilet paper. This captured the spirit of our boat perfectly. The *Eric* had been the scene of three previous shipboard weddings, but all of them had predated this captain and crew. Though neophytes, they really wanted this to be fun.

We climbed a steep set of stairs to the open-air top deck and stepped into our ceremony. Near a table toward the bow were our captain, Ivan Garay, and his first mate, Mario, in their crispest whites. Ivonne had stationed herself nearby, with three cameras strapped around her neck. The rest of our yacht-mates sat on beach chairs arranged in a semicircle. We were anchored a hundred or so yards from land, and among the swarm of birds that populated the island's cliffs were spots of brilliant red—the puffed chests of frigate birds. Some had managed to get airborne in their expanded state, as if they wished to get a closer view of the action aboard our boat.

Two fellow travelers, Nancy and Mary, volunteered to stand as witnesses for our ceremony. Both wore embroidered dresses, the Andean equivalent of Sunday finery, they'd purchased at a market near Machu Picchu. (Our fellow travelers had been touring together throughout South America for nearly three weeks already.) Ivan was nervous. After much arranging of places and clearing of throats, he began reading from our marriage license in halting English, then gave up and reverted to Spanish. Ivonne translated. We exchanged vows of our own invention (Sam: "I promise to evolve with you."), slipped rings on each other's heat-swollen fingers, and kissed—a universal punctuation mark. Sunset opposite the island provided a spectacular backdrop for a champagne toast. By the time we finally retired belowdecks for dinner, the moon hung in the night sky.

Dinner presented an opportunity for us to survey our fellow travelers, most of whom were of retirement age, for their insight into long and happy marriages. We sat first with Jim and Jacki, a retired general practitioner and dietitian, respectively, from Hood River, Oregon. How many years had they been married?

"Answer quick," Jacki said, turning to Jim.

"It will be fifty in 2004," Jim said, chuckling at his sleight of hand.

"Good answer," she nodded.

So, what's the secret?

"Develop common interests," Jacki said. "I see so many couples where the wife is focused on the kids and the husband is focused on his own thing, and they grow apart."

Jim nodded approvingly, and added, "I really believe in companionship. When I would go to medical conferences, she would

Lisa borrowed a blue handkerchief, and then remembered she already was wearing something blue—her boat shoes.

come with me. I really believe that anyone, regardless of moral stature, or religion, or standing in the community, is capable of doing something they really regret later. I know because they come see me to fix it!"

We tracked down Nancy, Lisa's maid of honor and still the life of the party well into her eighth decade. Nancy was a longtime divorcee, and her firsthand experience in these matters had been accumulated the hard way. Her advice was simple: "Keep your sense of humor."

We were invited to sit at the captain's table for dessert, a wedding cake that the staff had decorated with an icing rendition of lovestruck booby birds. The Ecuadorian national dessert is a layered sponge cake with alcohol-soaked filling that had made our faces swell with sugar when it was served with dinner on the flight from Miami. On this night, we each had an extra serving.

Four days and three nights aboard Ecoventura's *Eric* start at $1,275 per person, including all meals, guide services, and transportation within the Galápagos. Longer stays, and larger boats, also can be arranged. For more information contact Galápagos Network, 800-633-7972, or see www.wwb.com/company/c008393.html.

Blue-footed boobies were everywhere in the Galápagos, including atop our wedding cake.

La Mirage

A local travel agent arranged for us to visit Hosteria La Mirage, a small hotel in the Andean foothills an hour-and-a-half drive north of Quito that had received an ecstatic write-up in the guidebook we were carrying. What a call. Befitting its name, La Mirage is an oasis of elegance and quiet within easy striking distance of Ecuador's busiest outdoor market in Otavalo.

It's also romantic to the bone and a screaming bargain. We paid $190 for a night's stay, including dinner and breakfast the next morning. A stroll through La Mirage's flower-strewn grounds alone was worth the money. There were flowers floating in bowls on tabletops throughout the property, fountains of flowers in the main courtyard, flower petals on our canopy bed after it had been turned down for the night. In addition to the verdant landscape, clever architecture infuses each of La Mirage's twenty-three rooms with a palpable sense of privacy. Stellar meals, meticulously presented, sent our stay over the top.

The restaurant at La Mirage, like everything else on the property, is awash in flowers.

We milked every moment we had at La Mirage. Our visit included breakfast among the hummingbirds that inhabit the central garden, massages and aromatherapy treatments at the hotel spa, and a guided horseback ride through the surrounding town into the Andean foothills. Twenty-four hours did not do the place justice; a more appropriate stay would be in the two- to three-day range, which would be plenty of time to soak up La Mirage's ambiance and to make a few shopping forays into the surrounding countryside, the crafts capital of Ecuador.

For more information, call 011-593-6-915237 or E-mail lamirage@relaischateaux.fr.

Nuts and Bolts

Where to Start

The staff of the *Eric* was superaccommodating and friendly, but inexperienced with regard to weddings at sea. It may pay at the outset to enlist the help of Elvira de Kure, a wedding consultant based in Guayaquil who arranges ceremonies throughout Ecuador. For more information, call 011-593-4-323-557 or E-mail akure@gye.satnet.net.

Travel Information

Though a number of major carriers, including American, United, and Continental, service the international airport in Quito, we chose to fly Ecuadorian-owned Saeta Airlines—and enjoyed the carrier's democratic spirit immensely. At the counter, we asked about the possibility of flying first class. "The whole cabin is first class," was the Saeta employee's response, delivered with a sly smile. Saeta also connects Quito with the Galápagos via Guayaquil. For more information, call 305-341-8913.

Legal Requirements

To obtain a marriage license at sea, couples must provide their ship's captain with their passports, a certificate of nonimpediment to marriage from their local registrar translated into Spanish, and certified divorce decrees or death certificates, if applicable.

The ship's captain who marries you will provide an Act of Marriage at Sea Certificate, which you then present to the Registro Civil in San Cristóbal at the end of the cruise.

No immunizations are required. Malaria pills are necessary only if you plan to visit the rain forest (inland Ecuador).

Lead Time

You'll need one week to one month, depending on Ecoventura's availability. There is no residency requirement in Ecuador.

When to Go

The Galápagos' climate is largely determined by the ocean currents, which can be unpredictable. They generally run warmest from January to April and cooler June through November, during which time the islands are considerably less green. High tourist seasons are June through August and winter holidays.

Additional Contact Information

For information on Ecuador or the Galápagos, go to www .viaecuador.com on the Web.

Recommended Reading

The Beak of the Finch, by Jonathan Weiner, is an account of ongoing research in the Galápagos regarding the vagaries of natural selection. It manages somehow to make measuring birds' beaks a fascinating act. Take along *The Origin of Species* if you must, but it's a grinding read. Michael Jackson's *Galápagos: A Natural History* is the definitive naturalist's guide.

Cruises

Ocean journeys, from tall ships to transatlantic luxury liners, have tickled our collective fancy since we first crawled out of the primordial ooze somewhere down the evolutionary ladder. Even the (dare we say it?) ill-fated Titanic has demonstrated a certain allure in recent years.

The days of derring-do and dangerous liaisons on the high seas may be over, but "I do's" are still very much en vogue aboard cruise ships today. Here are three shipboard eloping options.

Princess Cruises

Cost: $$$$

Degree of difficulty: No sweat

Princess Cruises is the first cruise line to offer a complete onboard wedding while at sea. Most cruise lines can only perform ceremonies in port, either on land or while tied up to the pier. There's actually a wedding chapel, the first ever at sea, on board Princess Cruises's newest ship, the *Grand Princess*. The wedding chapel features stained glass, murals, and wood floors and is packed with flowers for weddings. There is room for a string quartet as well as guests.

But that's not the best part. All those romantic stories about couples falling in love on transatlantic crossings and being married by the captain of the ship? For ships registered in the United States, they're nothing more than folklore—a ship's captain can't marry anyone unless he's also a certified minister.

Aboard the *Grand Princess*, however, the romantic legend becomes truth: Liberia (where this particular behemoth is registered) recognizes the ship's captain as a legal officiant while at sea, and weddings aboard the *Grand Princess* are conducted by the man in the white hat.

Nuts and Bolts

Where to Start
Wedding options aboard the *Grand Princess* start at $1,400 and range up to $2,400—a figure that does not include the cost of the cruise itself. For more information, contact Princess Cruises at 800-421-1700 or see www.princess.com.

Travel Information
The *Grand Princess*, reportedly the biggest and most expensive cruise ship ever built, sails in the Caribbean during the fall, winter, and spring from Fort Lauderdale, Florida. The ship is in the Mediterranean during the summer months, sailing from either Barcelona or Istanbul.

Legal Requirements
Marriages conducted on the *Grand Princess* are performed by the captain under authority of Liberian maritime law. Both parties must be at least eighteen years old and have appropriate photo identification issued by a government authority (i.e., a passport, a driver's license, or an official identification card). Two adult witnesses are required.

Although a souvenir parchment wedding certificate is provided on board, the official marriage certificates are sent by Princess Cruises after you return home.

Lead Time
In theory, weddings aboard the *Grand Princess* can be booked up until the day before the ship sails, so long as you are already signed up for the cruise. If a wedding time is available and you have all the necessary paperwork with you, a ceremony can even be arranged while at sea. Just like in the movies!

Carnival Cruise Lines

Cost: $$$$

Degree of difficulty: No sweat

Some cruise lines, like Carnival, take advantage of spectacular ports of call to provide idyllic settings for their passengers' vows. In addition to the ease of planning a wedding with Carnival's help, couples get the experience of marrying in a beautiful tropical destination. It can be the best of both worlds.

Carnival weddings take place in Ocho Rios, Key West, Nassau, Catalina Island, San Juan, or Saint Thomas. In Ocho Rios, it's a tree-lined park complete with waterfall and tropical foliage; on Key West it's a private beach. Ditto Nassau, although the option of a flowery gazebo at the Radisson Beach Hotel also is available. In San Juan, couples get a taste of Puerto Rico's history at El Morro, overlooking the ocean, or they can opt for the tropical garden at the Caribe Hilton. Saint Thomas offers yet another tropical island for weddings.

The civil ceremony is generally kept brief; while tropical weddings are beautiful on warm sunny days, they also have a tendency to be, well, warm. A champagne toast and the cake cutting generally take place on site.

Carnival's shoreside weddings are arranged and timed for a bride and groom only, and transportation to and from the site is provided only for the couple. Expect an extra charge for any guests who want to attend.

Travel Tips for a Romantic Cruise

Two words: double bed. Another word: double-check. Cruise ship accommodations can be difficult to negotiate in advance, particularly when you want to make sure you've got the appropriate sleeping arrangements for your wedding night. Be sure to specify that you want a cabin with a double bed.

Two more words: private balcony. Staterooms with private balconies are more expensive than inside cabins, but the pleasure of standing together in the sea breeze, with distant islands on the horizon, far outweighs the expense.

Two final words: private dining. It's tricky to get that table for two, but it can be done. Private balconies are one way around the group seating situations often found on cruise ships—just order room service and dine outdoors. If you really need to get out of your cabin for a meal, call the higher-end restaurants. You should be able to score a table for two with an advance reservation. Dining during "off-peak" hours when other passengers are either getting ready for dinner or heading off to bed also can help keep the communal table phenomenon at bay.

Nuts and Bolts

Where to Start

Carnival Cruise Line offers numerous wedding package options both onboard and on land, starting at around $550. Again, this fee is above and beyond the cost of the cruise itself. For more information, call 800-933-4968, or see www.carnival.com.

Travel Information

Most Carnival cruises depart from Miami. Check with the line for details on your destination's departure city.

Legal Requirements

You are responsible for obtaining your own marriage license from the country in which the wedding is performed, and regulations vary depending on which wedding site you choose. Carnival is available to assist with the red tape.

Lead Time

Carnival wedding reservations are made on a first come, first served basis and can't be booked until after the cruise reservation is confirmed. Book your cruise and wedding at least thirty-five days prior to setting sail to assure yourselves that you complete the necessary legal requirements in time.

Take Our Advice

Ever wonder why cruise ships insist on providing their wedding parties with flowers? Blame U.S. Customs's agricultural regulations: passengers can't bring their own flowers on board the ship. So if you've had your heart set on a particular bouquet with which to elope, be prepared and have it done in silk before you leave.

American Hawaii Cruises

Cost: $$

Degree of difficulty: Moderate

If your hearts are set on marrying in Hawaii, but you want the ease of a shipboard wedding, American Hawaii Cruises offers both. Romance in Paradise packages include a three-, four-, or seven-day cruise and a ceremony in, obviously, paradise.

Couples may be married on board at port at any stop along the way. Weddings on the bridge of the ship in Kona enjoy a view of the picturesque fishing village. Local ministers or justices of the peace officiate. Music is provided by one of Hawaii's ubiquitous ukeleleists.

American Hawaii schedules just three weddings per weekly sailing and only one per day. While this limits your options somewhat (weddings take place on specific days at specific times in specific ports of call), it also guarantees you special attention.

Nuts and Bolts

Where to Start

American Hawaii Cruises offers a standard wedding package for $595. Two add-on romance packages are highly recommended. The Honi-Honi (Hawaiian Kisses) is $595 and includes his and hers souvenir robes, tropical flowers, champagne and strawberries, keepsake champagne flutes, a souvenir photograph, a travel diary, a limousine transfer to the ship, and a lei greeting. The Ku'uipo (Island Sweethearts) package is $295 and provides his and hers massages, a private candlelit dinner (complete with Hawaiian serenade), and a convertible car rental on the island of your choice. The two add-ons can be combined for $875. For more information, call American Hawaii Cruises at 800-513-5022 or visit www.cruisehawaii.com.

Travel Information

American Hawaii Cruises sails exclusively in the Hawaiian islands out of its home base in Honolulu.

Lead Time

Because American Hawaii chooses to do relatively few weddings aboard ship—and because the rooms with double beds fill up extra fast—it's recommended that you book as much as ninety days prior to sailing. American Hawaii cruises can deal with far shorter notice, however, according to availability.

Part V

Elsewhere

Here we use the term *elsewhere* to mean "places where it's possible to elope that don't fit into tidy categories for the purposes of this book." It's in no way meant as a slight. In fact, the two places in this section that we experienced firsthand—Israel and Kenya—rank at the very top of our favorite experiences the

entire year we spent researching *Beyond Vegas*. (We loved them all, of course, but the urge to rank is irresistible.)

When you elope someplace so exotic as Kenya, everything that's even remotely familiar is stripped away. The sun rises in the wrong direction, and

the water circles the wrong way around the drain. What's left is just the two of you, alone, with little to concentrate on besides one another. The sense of teamwork that true travel engenders is nothing if not romantic. We encourage you to go see for yourselves.

Israel

Cost: $$

Degree of Difficulty: Doable

Israelis are a pragmatic breed. Which may explain why so many citizens expressed surprise at our desire to elope in their country. Apparently everyday life is too fraught with the threat of civil unrest, too burdened by the limitations of a nascent economy, for the locals to view their country as idealistically as we did. You hear a lot of grumbling during a trip to Israel.

But not far beneath the surface is a wellspring of enormous pride, upon which the Jewish State has drawn several times to defend its borders during Israel's half-century in existence. For Jews such as ourselves, this is a romantic notion.

The most compelling reason to visit Israel, regardless of religion, is that it's so darn old. In the last four thousand years, great empires have waxed and waned over this slice of Mediterranean shoreline, eroding the landscape to stone (contemporary Israelis take considerable pride in their attempts to beautify their terrain with frenzied plantings of fast-growing pine trees). Here it is possible to stand in one spot and know that the earliest Jews (Israelites), then Babylonians, then Greeks, then Romans, then Byzantines, then Crusaders, then Moslems, then Ottomans, then British, then Jordanians, now Jews again all beat you to it. The

In Israel, no wedding is complete without an outbreak of dancing.

unmistakable moral of the story: live for the moment, because everything that feels permanent is in fact entirely mutable.

For Jews, eloping in Israel is a bit complicated, however. The line between politics and religion in the Jewish State, like the back edge of the batter's box at Fenway Park by the bottom of the third inning of a game, has been obliterated by partisans angling for an edge. Everything is political in Israel, even weddings: at the time of our visit, Orthodox rabbis maintained a stranglehold on Israel's "official" Jewish rituals, including marriages. There are Orthodox rabbis who will marry couples on the fly, but only after the bride and groom have navigated the paperwork stateside. What's more, Orthodox protocol is not for everybody.

There are, of course, ways around this. Israelis who don't identify with the Orthodox movement often are legally married in Cyprus—a matter of a short flight or cruise and a few hundred dollars—then return home for a religious ceremony with a non-Orthodox rabbi attended by friends and family. We did an Americanized version of the same, arriving in Israel with a marriage certificate already in hand and then enlisting a Reform rabbi to perform a special and celebratory, though not legally binding, wedding in Jerusalem.

This was surprisingly easy to accomplish on our own, once we learned how to leverage the political system to our advantage. Within three phone calls from the States we connected with Rabbi Michael Boyden, a member of the Israel Council of Progressive Rabbis, an association of thirty to thirty-five rabbis intent on providing a liberal Jewish alternative to the Orthodox way. He was glad to handle our wedding ceremony on principle alone; the wackier our circumstance, the better so far as his cause was concerned. Again, everything in Israel is political.

All Rabbi Boyden asked of us in return was that we show him an existing marriage certificate, our passports, and a letter from a local rabbi near our home in San Francisco attesting to our status "as respected members of the Jewish community" (i.e., confirming that we were both Jewish). During our initial conversation, he was happy to leave the exact date, time, and location of our ceremony within Jerusalem up in the air until we arrived later that month. Had we wished to be married in a cable car on our way up to the elevated fortress at Masada, or in a marketplace, or underwater in scuba gear in the Red Sea, Rabbi Boyden probably would have gone along with that too. We'd clearly found the right guy.

• • • • •

Within a few days of arriving in Israel, we met with Rabbi Boyden at his large and modern home in suburban Hod Hasharon. Over coffee and a plate of sugar cookies—an Israeli staple—we discussed the logistics of our ceremony and circumstances that fueled the Council of Progressive Rabbis' zeal. One issue was the katubah, the contract to which Jewish brides traditionally affix their name immediately prior to their ceremony. The Orthodox rabbinate uses a standard katubah that refers to the wife's virginity as a commodity that is being purchased and determines the size of the sum she will receive in the event her husband decides to divorce her. "We use a katubah which reflects the egalitarian nature of marriage in modern society," Boyden said. Then he broke out a copy of our katubah for us to peruse. Indeed, it was groovy.

Another issue is the giving of a ring. In Orthodox ceremonies, the ring is viewed as the bridal price given by the groom to the bride. In the ceremonies that Rabbi Boyden and his colleagues officiate, rings are exchanged by the couple.

Perhaps most onerous to the Council of Progressive Rabbis is Israelis' lack of choice in the matter. Orthodox Jews are in fact a minority of the population, but a well-organized and politically fervent one that enjoys outsized clout. If Boyden and Company get their way, all Israelis will enjoy the right to marry in a manner that jibes with their beliefs.

As for our own wedding, our hearts were set on the Old City in Jerusalem for religious and historical resonance. But we continued to leave the specific spot at which to stage our ceremony up in the air. Our hope was that a sense of spontaneous celebration would sweep the logistics along in a momentum entirely their own. And they did.

• • • • •

There has been a citadel on the site of the Tower of David for two thousand years.

The day of our ceremony, we gathered the raw materials for a Jewish wedding: wine, *kippahs* for covering the men's heads, and a glass wrapped in a napkin. Rabbi Boyden would bring the *huppah*—a ceremonial tent traditionally held over Jewish couples during their wedding. Here's a tip: regardless of which wine happens to be your preference, go with a screw-top bottle. Flavor is not nearly the same priority as ease of use when it comes to weddings.

We stood at our designated meeting place, Dung Gate—one of eight entranceways into the Old City—and waited for Rabbi Boyden to arrive. Standing beneath the stone archway added to our already palpable sense of awe. "Jerusalem syndrome," in which the vibe of the place temporarily overwhelms your faculties and you begin believing you are a character from the Bible, reportedly afflicts several hundred visitors per year. The number is believable when you're there.

Rabbi Boyden met us at 10 A.M., and we set out in search of a site for our ceremony. The tight expression on Rabbi Boyden's face that morning was part bemusement, part concentration. It was perhaps forty degrees, with a chill wind that accelerated among the Old City's narrow streets and cut through our clothes without sympathy.

The Tower of David Museum, near Jaffa Gate, fit our criteria perfectly. It is semisecluded, away from the ultrareligious throng that gathers at the Western Wall—the most sacred site in the entire Jewish world—and has been known to hassle less Orthodox souls such as ourselves. The museum is also ancient and historically significant. The structure originally was fortified by Herod the Great between 37 and 34 B.C., a period of frenzied development throughout Israel. Herod was an ambitious (some would say maniacal) builder, whose palaces and palisades have been unearthed in all corners of the country. A succession of occupants alternately razed and rebuilt the citadel, most notably Sultan Suleiman the Magnificent in the mid-sixteenth century. The gate, stone bridge, and western terrace that comprise the bulk of the museum today are all legacies of the Ottoman Empire, but the massive bricks from which they're constructed were hewn by Herod. Jerusalem is big on recycling that way.

The Tower of David Museum also had an ideal outdoor spot for our ceremony—an intimate courtyard with an herb garden and a solitary olive tree—and a nearby sitting room in which we could change in and out of our wedding clothes and warm up over trays of cafeteria hot chocolate, so long as we didn't mind sharing the space with a group of forty or so Israeli Army soldiers who happened to be touring the facility that day. No problem.

In the sitting room Rabbi Boyden broke out a copy of our katubah for us to sign. Then the wedding party, which included Lisa's brother, Kevin, his wife, Caron, and their three-year-old daughter, Shai, gathered up its cups of hot chocolate and moved outside.

One of Israel's most shocking qualities is its small scale: the entire country could fit within New Jersey's borders. While touring the countryside, the density of the cultural, religious, and physical landmarks—as well as the profusion of ancient but diminutive olive trees—shrinks the proportions even further. This sense of constricted physical space acts to intensify events, and emotions run closer to the surface here for better and for worse. In our case this worked to our advantage; our wedding took on an outsized sense of celebration. We invited four of the uniformed Israeli Army officers to hold our *huppah*. While Rabbi Boyden assembled the poles from a kit in his briefcase, the officers donned colorful berets denoting their military specialty. The rest of the soldiers—men and women—gathered around us in a spontaneous throng.

Drinking wine is a major theme in many Jewish rituals.

Jewish wedding ceremonies usually are short and sweet. Outdoor Jewish weddings in Jerusalem in wintertime are especially so. Rabbi Boyden said a few welcoming words and recounted an ancient prophecy made by the prophet Jeremiah following the dispersion of the first Jewish state in ancient times, that Jews would one day return to Jerusalem and the city would "rejoice with the sound of the bride and the bridegroom." On this day, that was us.

From there the ceremony only picked up steam. We unscrewed the top off our wine and drank from a shared cup while Rabbi

Boyden intoned a blessing in Hebrew. In keeping with Jewish custom, we placed the rings on each other's right index fingers.

Rabbi Boyden read from our katubah in Hebrew and in English and offered seven traditional blessings. And then he presented the glass. Stateside, shattering a glass wrapped in cloth at the conclusion of a Jewish wedding ceremony is said to signify any number of things, from fertility to remembrance of the Holocaust. In Israel, it's a no-brainer: it's about the destruction of the second temple in the year A.D. 70 at the hands of Roman marauders. Rabbi Boyden placed the bundled glass on the ground before us and had Sam repeat in pidgin Hebrew, "If I forget thee, O Jerusalem, let my right hand

Our ring bearer, Shai, was an inveterate ham.

forget its cunning . . . ," meaning even at weddings we do not forget the destruction of Jerusalem. Then he invited Sam to give it a stomp. The resulting crunch may well have echoed off the Temple's ruined walls mere yards from where we stood.

We'll never know. Immediately the courtyard filled with shouting and spontaneous dancing. Rabbi Boyden and the *huppah*-holding officers linked hands and circled around us in a whirl of military green, while the rest of the squad—and several tourists on a balcony above—clapped in syncopated rhythm. Lisa's first attempt at tossing her bouquet landed at her feet: the winter wind knocked it off course, she later claimed. Her second attempt ended up nestled safely in the arms of a young woman in olive fatigues. Mazel Tov!

You can rent the Tower of David Museum for $500 a pop. For more information, call 011-972-2-6265333.

Making it Legal

Orthodox Jewish Weddings

Jewish couples must be married by an Orthodox rabbi in the Torah tradition for their ceremony to be recognized by the state of Israel. There is no such thing as a civil ceremony in Israel.

To be married by an Orthodox rabbi, first you'll need to contact the rabbinate nearest the town where you wish to get married. Contact information for specific rabbinates is available by calling 011-972-2-5388605. Or see the Ministry of Religion's website at www.religinfoserv.gov.il. Click on "computerized information services" and then "services," where you will find wedding laws and local contact buttons.

There is no set waiting period, but you will need to arrange for a sequence of events with the rabbi to whom you are assigned by the local rabbinate. Generally speaking, you should be able to tie the knot within a week after arriving in Israel.

Couples must provide a letter from an Orthodox rabbi back home stating that they are indeed both Jewish and attesting that they never have been married, or that they received a kosher Jewish divorce (*gett*) by an Orthodox rabbinical court in America.

Brides must attend a *mikva* for their ritual cleansing prior to their ceremony. In Israel, this usually is done the night before the wedding. The rabbi or local rabbinate will tell you where to go. If you do this in the States, be sure to bring a letter documenting your attendance.

After your ceremony, your marriage papers must be filed in person at the local rabbinate.

Christian Weddings

Getting married as a Christian in Israel is a lot easier than getting married as a Jew in Israel. Many Christian denominations are "recognized" religious communities by the state. These include Greek Orthodox, (Melkite) Greek Catholic, Latin, Armenian Orthodox, Syrian Catholic, Chaldean Catholic, Maronite, Syrian Orthodox, Armenian Catholic, and (Anglican) Evangelical Episcopal. For historical reasons dating from Ottoman times, the ecclesiastical courts of these communities are granted jurisdiction in matters of personal status, such as marriage and divorce. In other words, each church is free to legally marry its minions however it sees fit.

The first thing you'll need to do is contact your church in Israel. The Christian Information Centre in Jerusalem (phone 011-972-2-6272692) has phone numbers for all the various denominations. Another resource is ITAF tour company, which arranges Christian as well as Jewish weddings in Israel (phone 800-326-4827).

Elsewhere in Israel

There are plenty of holy sites for everyone in Israel. The following are some wedding-appropriate places of religious significance for Christians. We've also included some accommodations and

Druze Homestay

The Druze are an ethnic minority largely concentrated within Israel in a few villages near the Sea of Galilee. Though the Druze keep their religion strictly under wraps, their cuisine is available for anyone to sample in the town of Daliat El Carmel, where several families have opened their doors to visitors for traditional meals.

Be sure to arrive on time; your host family will have been preparing for your arrival for a week, and everything is synchronized toward the exact moment when dozens of piping hot dishes hit the table all at once. During our visit, every square inch of our table was filled with Druze specialties such as rice wrapped with grape leaves. That and a bottle of 7-Up.

After the meal we were invited into our host family's pillow-strewn reclining room to sip spicy Druze coffee, nibble honey-saturated pastries (think baklava), and have our coffee grounds read by the matriarch of the house. As she settled into position, tucking her legs beneath her on the cold floor (this back room was so cold we could see our breath), we had our doubts. But right away she hit a home run: she nailed our guide, Yuval. Though we couldn't understand exactly what she was saying until later, the amazed expression on Yuval's face spoke volumes.

For more information regarding Druze homestays, call the Israeli Tourism Bureau at 888-77-ISRAEL (888-774-7723).

restaurants you might want to consider for the honeymoon portion of your stay.

Cana

The little village of Kfar Cana on the Sea of Galilee near Nazareth is identified as the site where Jesus performed his first miracle of converting water into wine—at a wedding! Many young couples are married at the Church of the Miracle, which is built on the ruins of a church built in the sixth century A.D. on this site.

Church of the Beatitudes

The Mount of Beatitudes overlooking the Sea of Galilee is where Christ is alleged to have fed five thousand people with five loaves and two fish, and where he delivered the Sermon on the Mount. The present-day Church of the Beatitudes was built on this site in 1937. Picture windows in its gallery enjoy some of the best views of the Sea of Galilee.

Mount of Olives

The Garden of Gethsemane, at the foot of the Mount of Olives in Jerusalem, is home to a stand of ancient olive trees that may well have been alive during Christ's last prayers on the site before his crucifixion. The garden is maintained by Franciscan monks.

Bethlehem

The Church of the Nativity in Bethlehem is built where it is believed Christ was born. It also happens to be one of the oldest churches in Israel; its basic structure was originally built in A.D. 530.

Favorite Honeymoon Spots

A honeymoon in Israel can revolve around the spiritual power of the place or its cultural wealth—or even adventure sports and spa living. During our trip we visited several luxurious and restful destinations that are ideally suited for postnuptial R&R.

In the village of Rosh Pina near the Sea of Galilee in northern Israel, we stayed one night at a spa, Mizpe Hayamim (phone 011-972-6-6999666, or fax 011-972-6-6999555). It features a variety of massage, aromatherapy, and body work options available by appointment, and a glass-enclosed hot tub overlooking the valley below. It happened to snow—an especially romantic (and rare) treat—while we enjoyed an excellent dinner at a local inn, Auberge Shulamit (phone 011-972-6-693-1485).

In southern Israel, on the shores of the Dead Sea, is a series of spas that capitalize on the region's healthful natural environment. Mineral-rich Dead Sea mud is reputed to have a variety of beneficial effects; Lisa swears her arthritic knee felt better after a treatment. The Dead Sea also happens to be four hundred meters below sea level, and the extraoxygenated air and filtered ozone are great for the complexion. We stayed at the ultramodern Hyatt Regency Dead Sea Resort and Spa and enjoyed double-barreled mud treatments (contact information is available at 011-972-7-6591234).

Israeli haute cuisine is a work in progress. The good stuff is found at roadside falafel stands that line almost every city street. The single best meal we had in all of Israel consisted of little more than flat bread and marjoram toasted in a clay oven, served with a bowl of olives. You have to taste fresh-ground marjoram to believe it.

We did enjoy a "nouvelle Israeli" (our term, not theirs) meal at Arcadia in Jerusalem (10 Agripas St., phone 011-972-2-6249138). Eucalyptus (7 Horkanos, phone 011-972-2-6244331), also in Jerusalem, is worth checking out for owner/cook Moshe Basson's theatrical dining room displays alone. Philadelphia, in the Arab quarter, set down a killer spread of traditional *mazzas* (appetizer-sized plates) for our wedding reception.

Tel Aviv, on the Mediterranean Sea, is a thoroughly modern city with a lively night scene and a number of ambitious restaurants. Honeymooners looking for the ultimate intimate dinner should check out the wine cellar at Prego Restaurant (9 Rothschild Blvd., phone 011-972-3-5179545), which barely has room for one table, two chairs, and an air conditioner to keep the wine cool.

Back in Jerusalem

The King David Hotel (011-972-2-6208888) in Jerusalem is among the nicest in all of Israel and routinely plays host to visiting diplomats, royalty, and the like. Rooms start at approximately $250. A former palace, The American Colony Hotel (011-972-2-627977) in East Jerusalem is a little artsier and more intimate, and is favored by movie stars and writer types. Rooms here are in the $175 to $200 range.

Jerusalem also is riddled with intimate hostels and bed-and-breakfasts, some of which have sheltered pilgrims of various denominations for centuries. We checked out Saint Andrew's Hospice, which sits behind the British Consul directly across a narrow valley from the Old City, and found it hushed and interesting (phone 011-972-2-6732401).

Nuts and Bolts

Where to Start

Non-legally recognized (read, Reform) Jewish wedding ceremonies are considerably easier to pull together on your own than are Orthodox ones. Supercool Rabbi Boyden is an excellent place to start. To reach him, phone: 011-972-9-7463447, fax 011-972-9-7463448, or E-mail boyden@internet-zahav.net.

Legal weddings in Israel can be organized without the help of a wedding coordinator, but the process requires some patience. If you'd like a hand, here are some suggestions.

Rabbi Jay Karzen is an Orthodox rabbi in Jerusalem who specializes in bar and bat mitzvahs, and legal weddings for visitors. For a fee, he'll help couples find the perfect site for their ceremony as well as arrange for the photographer and videographer, flowers, music, et cetera—and officiate, of course. For more information, call 011-972-2-5631018, E-mail jkarzen@netvision.net.il, or see www.Israelvisit.co.il:80/.

ITAF is a U.S.–based bar mitzvah tour company that has handled some extraordinary wedding ceremonies as well. For more information, contact 800-326-4827.

Travel Information

In addition to offering direct service to Ben-Gurion Airport near Tel Aviv from Newark, New York, Miami, Baltimore–Washington, D.C., Chicago, and Los Angeles, El Al Israel Airlines is the standard against which airline security is measured throughout the world. Arrive extra early for your flight, and be prepared to face a rigorous interview while waiting in line for your boarding pass. For more information, contact El Al at 800-223-6700.

Legal Requirements

There are no requirements per se to conduct a non-legally recognized wedding ceremony in Israel. All Rabbi Boyden asked to see were copies of an existing wedding certificate and our passports. He also asks couples who intend to complete the process in reverse order—have their legal wedding after visiting Israel—to sign a declaration to the effect that they pledge to conduct a civil ceremony within less than a month.

Specifics for Orthodox Jewish and Christian ceremonies are given on pages 232 through 233.

Lead Time
Though Rabbi Boyden requires no set amount of advance notice, he is a busy man. The more notice you give, the more flexible he will be.

When to Go
Jerusalem is warmest (upward of eighty-five degrees) and driest in July and August, which also coincides with the high tourist season. In late spring or early fall you're likely to get the best mix of pleasant weather and thin crowds, but watch out for religious holidays (Passover, Easter, Yom Kippur, etc.), during which the city may become choked with pilgrims.

Additional Contact Information
For general information about vacationing in Israel, call the Israel Ministry of Tourism at 888-77-ISRAEL (888-774-7723).

Take Our Advice
Everything in Israel is political, and weddings are no exception. Jerusalem is especially charged. We heard stories of couples who held non-Orthodox ceremonies within sight of the Wailing Wall and were spit on by self-appointed ultrareligious decorum police who patrol the area (we experienced no hostility ourselves). The moral of the story: choose your site carefully, and rely on local wisdom/insight for guidance.

Israel begs for interpretation. Touring without the help of a trained guide can be confusing at best, overwhelming at worst. We enthusiastically recommend Yuval Russ (phone 011-972-52-

237714, or fax 011-972-9-796-7761), the top gun of Israeli tour guides. For $350 a day you get the use of Yuval's van (which seats ten people total) and access to his bottomless well of insight and humor. The Israel Ministry of Tourism and most Israel-centric travel agents also can help arrange for tour guides.

Recommended Reading

The New York Times is a good place to start reading up on contemporary Israel. Stephen Brooks's *Winner Takes All* and David Shipler's *Arab and Jew: Wounded Spirits in a Promised Land* also provide valuable context. Jerome Murphy-O'Conner's *The Holy Land* goes deep into the region's archaeological and biblical history.

Kenya

Cost: $$$

Degree of difficulty: Doable

There is a tidy little pagoda on the grounds of the Mount Kenya Safari Club, not unlike the whitewashed bandstands found on town commons throughout middle America. The structure is available for weddings.

But if you're going to travel all the way to East Africa to elope, it doesn't make sense to default to something familiar once you get there. Better to bypass the Mount Kenya Safari Club lawn and stage your ceremony in the bush, where a curious elephant might wander in. Charter a plane out of *Out of Africa* to whisk you from your hotel to the altar. Invite a choir and some Chuka tribesmen to bang out a tune on their goatskin drums. This was our experience, and it was a wild ride, alternately thrilling and pacifying to a degree that muddles our recollection of the event. But here goes.

· · · · ·

The Mount Kenya Safari Club is an apt place to spend your wedding day. Part of its romance is explained by the physical beauty of the place. The club is located on a ridge facing Mount Kenya, an extinct volcano from which the country derives its name. Guests can stand at the front entrance and absorb a view that

The site of our bush wedding was a clearing by a river shaded by yellow fever trees.

includes the club's own peacock-strewn lawn, foothills covered with conifer plantations and windswept plains (once a literal stomping ground for elephant herds numbering in the hundreds), and the mountain itself. As 17,058-foot summits go, Mount Kenya is one of the most clandestine you'll ever see. Or miss. One moment, it is obscured by mist and sheets of rain. The next, sun lends the scene an eerie clarity, foreshortening the distance between you and the glaciers that coat its twin summits.

When it comes to matters of the heart, the Mount Kenya Safari Club also has what might winkingly be referred to as a history. The original lodge was designed by wealthy New York socialite Rhoda Prudhomme as a gift for her young husband Gabriel. Prudhomme was a fifty-year-old matron with a taste for big game hunting; he was a dashing, young (emphasis on young)

French aviator who accompanied her on frequent forays into the bush. Their romance was quite the scandal among the festive "Happy Valley" set that frequented the Mount Kenya region immediately after World War I.

The club today resembles a cross between a lavish love nest—Ms. Prudhomme's handiwork, it is presumed—and a macho hunting lodge with a conspicuously glitzy bent. Movie star William Holden bought the property in 1959 and turned it into a see-and-be-seen stopover for the Hollywood crowd. Bing Crosby, Bob Hope, Conrad Hilton, and Lord Mountbatten were among the club's founding members.

Though the embers of the Happy Valley's once white-hot social scene have long since cooled, much about the Mount Kenya Safari Club still feels like a Rudyard Kipling novel sprung to life. A large measure of the club's charm lies in its enforced formality. Dinner at either of its two dining rooms is a jacket-required affair, expertly attended to by adult waiters in crimson coats. The food arrives in waves, each course presented, lightly commented upon, and then cleared before the next arrives. The night before our wedding, we awakened our appetites with canapés and gimlets served by a fireplace in the taxidermy-heavy main lodge, then settled into comfortable leather chairs in one of the safari club's two dining rooms for a belt-popping meal.

• • • • •

The next morning, we made a last-ditch attempt at some semblance of a traditional wedding day. After breakfast in the main hall, Lisa indulged in a facial and massage while Sam headed straight for the golf course. Built by Holden in the early 1960s, the nine-hole par 3 circuit makes clever use of limited space by tucking several greens around, through, and occasionally behind exotic trees that are just tall enough to scale with the right club. Caddies are a must. The course also is notable for its fauna, including peacocks, the Mount Kenya Safari Club's unofficial mascots. The weather that day was typically stellar; central Kenya's climate varies from pleasantly springlike to perfect, with a perpetually bright sun that somehow is cooler than its intensity suggests.

Lisa's morning included an impromptu relationship counseling session with the women who provided her manicure and massage. As it turns out, formal marriage is a withering institution among Kenyans. For many, the cost of staging a large wedding is prohibitive—and there's no such thing as a small wedding in Kenya. It's all or nothing and, increasingly, Kenyans are opting for the latter. Traditional tribal ceremonies that bind couples in the eyes of their contemporaries but are not officially recognized by the state also are popular.

Midafternoon, we returned to our suite to put ourselves together for the ceremony. Keeping the groom from seeing the bride is not so easy when you elope. We passed hairbrushes and garment bags around cracked doors, but violations were inevitable. Around 5 P.M. the Mount Kenya Safari Club's general manager, St. John ("Sinjin") Kelliher, appeared at our door to summon us for our ceremony.

A gregarious sort, Sinjin had personally arranged all our wedding logistics, and apparently had taken to heart our encouragement that he err on the side of the sensational. First stop for us was a dirt runway minutes from the safari club via Land Rover. In the clearing stood a gleaming silver vintage plane, waiting to whisk us to the spot in the bush where our ceremony was to take place. Sinjin's wife, Karen, waited for us beneath one of the wings.

Our pilot, Jim from Minneapolis, had grown bored flying corporate jets in the United States, and moved to rural Kenya to

For weddings in the bush, they really roll out the red carpet.

launch a charter tour business. Jim had an appropriate flair for the dramatic. Prior to takeoff he produced a tin from a pocket within his jumpsuit and offered us lemon drops. Once airborne, he piped the string-laden soundtrack to *Out of Africa* through our headsets while flying enervatingly low above the wheat-colored landscape, which was dotted by haunchy zebras and green-lidded yellow fever trees. Moments before touchdown he buzzed the landing strip theatrically to scare a herd of warthogs out of their potholes. As spectacular entrances go, James Brown himself would be hard-pressed to top that one. We emerged from the fuselage grinning from ear to ear.

The spot Sinjin had chosen for our ceremony in the bush was shaded by a canopy of yellow fever trees, whose spidery beauty belies their ghastly name. On the ground was a clean red carpet leading to a mahogany desk, behind which sat a round-faced district officer who'd been summoned from the nearest town to conduct the civil half of our ceremony. Weeks later, while looking at photos of that day, we noticed an unfortunate lion pelt at the foot of the district officer's desk, and two huge elephant tusks framing either side like giant parentheses. At the moment of our arrival in the bush, however, the details of the scene were a bit of a blur.

Our entrance was greeted by the rhythmic pounding of a dozen Chuka drummers, the traditional "keepers" of nearby Mount Kenya. They sounded three beats—boom, boom, boom—then shouted, "*Karibu!*" (it means welcome) in unison until we reached our seats at the end of the red carpet. A choir of young men and women, arranged in rows, women in front, sang in Swahili once the drumming ceased and before the vow-making, ring-exchanging, and paper-signing started. Their precision was effortless, the blend of voices delicate and pretty. It was near sunset. The pendulum swung; we both felt a thorough and surprising sense of calm, despite the whirl of activity that surrounded us.

We exchanged our own vows, which we had hastily scrawled on scraps of paper in the hotel suite that afternoon. At the district officer's urging, we slipped rings of yellow Masai beads on each other's fingers. We approached the desk and signed our marriage certificate. We stood for the district officer's advice, dispensed in perfect English: "Respect your partner. No polygamy. Enjoy the day. You may kiss the bride." The soothing effect of the sound of wind in acacia trees was considerable.

Then it was the Chuka drummers' turn to kick up their heels in earnest. Their chief, Ali, stepped forward to deliver his blessing while his fellow tribesmen formed a circle around us. Feathers arranged like wings on Ali's forearms gently fanned our faces as he wove a fantastic tale about our lives together, in Swahili, draw-

After the civil ceremony, the Chuka tribesmen performed a blessing ceremony.

ing giggles from the women in the choir when he pointed to Lisa and pantomimed a pregnant belly. The meaning was obvious, though we understood not a word of what he said.

Ali stepped back with the other drummers in the circle, which began to slowly rotate around us. Following inscrutable cues, the drummers would interrupt their rhythm midbeat to blow aluminum whistles and holler. If you squint a bit, a circle of hollering Chuka drummers is not unlike celebrants at a Jewish wedding dancing the hora. A party is a party, and the bodily reflex is the same: adrenaline.

Sinjin gestured for us to be seated again for more singing by the Swahili choir. Their tune was less delicate this time, more peppy. One of the women in the choir plucked a finger harp. Its sharp notes blended with the choir's tidy harmonies and the sound

Your basic giraffe

of the breeze in the acacia trees. The adrenaline generated by the Chuka dancers dissipated in our bloodstream and again we felt thoroughly serene.

Our exit was less spectacular than our airborne entrance, but at that point we were ready for something more earthly anyway. Sinjin escorted us back to the Land Rover for a postceremony game drive. We paused at a clearing where baboons and gazelles gathered en masse. Though the elephants in the area had steered clear of our ceremony, we discovered several lingering here. There's no understating how mesmerizing it is to see an elephant or a giraffe (or dik-dik, or hippo, or warthog) in its natural environment. That these animals still exist in the wild is a source of deep joy. We never got over it our entire time in Kenya.

Our destination was another tree-shaded spot along the river, where a table had been prepared for our celebratory dinner. A bonfire eased the transition from sunset into chilly night, and the last rays of the day filtered through the smoke. Sinjin and Karen joined us for a champagne toast, then bid us farewell with hearty handshakes and left us to our meal—but not alone. A pair of eland, giant antelope with thin white stripes on their backs, materialized in the twilight and maneuvered into the river for a drink.

Walk, Don't Ride

Tourists, conditioned by the images that appear in *National Geographic* and on the Discovery Channel to expect intimate access to fish and fowl, arrive in Kenya with checklists of animals they wish to see, and a sense that anything less than petting distance would be a gip. As a consequence, vast areas of the bush are marred by Land Rover tracks, and prides of lions spend the bulk of each day surrounded on all sides by lenses. At the Mara Safari Club near the Masai Mara National Reserve in southwest Kenya, we literally got caught in a traffic jam during a morning game drive in the bush.

A far better option is to leave the Land Rover in the garage and embark on foot—with the aid of a resident naturalist, of course. And an armed guard or two. We took a half-dozen such walks in the bush during our stay in Kenya and experienced just one moment of danger: Lisa somehow managed to hook a crocodile while fishing for catfish. The fearsome beast severed the line before ever reaching the shore. It should be noted that Lisa never lost her grip on the reel, however, even while the rest of our party—including an armed ranger—were backpedaling double time.

Otherwise, walking safaris felt safe and were exhilarating in a way that tearing around the bush in a vehicle cannot conjure. During our stay at Galdessa (discussed later) we toured a section of Tsavo East National Park in which the Kenya Wildlife Service is attempting to reintroduce black rhinos, poached virtually to extinction throughout the continent. A ranger from the rhino project, Christopher Ruta, accompanied us during our four-hour trek, which wandered through dry riverbeds and thickets of acacia trees. He was tracking a specific rhino, Maria, with whom he was on a first-name basis thanks to the reintroduction program.

At an incongruously green lagoon amid the reddish countryside, Ruta paused to point out a pair of macaw birds on a branch overhead and the elaborate home of a family of weaver birds. Elsewhere we examined anthills the size and shape of outhouses, and tidy piles of dung left by diminutive dik-diks. "This is how they trap a rhino," Ruta commented, pointing at a small pyramid of pellets. It took a moment for the joke to sink in.

Occasionally we'd spy a giraffe in the distance or hear an elephant's rumbling stomach. But Maria remained scarce until the very end. After four hours in the bush, Ruta finally spied her within a few hundred yards of our camp. He gestured for us to follow him and to mimic his cautious crouch. A startled rhino is among the most dangerous animals in all of Africa.

To calm her nerves, Ruta called to Maria by name. Raised in a pen at a nearby ranger station, she had lived successfully in the wild for more than a year but remained attached to her surrogate parents.

"Does she recognize your voice specifically?" we asked Ruta, now standing within forty feet of the prehistoric-looking beast.

"I don't know," Ruta replied. "We've never talked about it."

As omens go, our wedding day ended with a doozy. En route back to the safari club we spotted (with the help of a searchlight) a silver-backed jackal nursing a litter of pups. For several long moments we gaped silently while the young jackals jockeyed for position beneath their mother's stomach. Then our chaperone, Lonrho Hotels naturalist Jama Suleiman—a former Kenya Wildlife Service ranger who had literally fought wars to protect the region's resident animals—was moved to break the silence: "I've never seen that before."

The Mount Kenya Safari Club's two hundred-plus villas, cottages, suites, and club rooms all enjoy views of the summit (weather permitting, of course). Rooms start at $360, including all meals. For more information, call 800-845-3692.

Our reception, like our ceremony, was held in the bush.

Mukutan and Galdessa

Bush lodges are the Kenyan equivalent of staying at a bed-and-breakfast. Fewer guests mean steeper fees. But there's a payoff: spectacular service and an otherworldly sense of isolation. We stayed at two such lodges, Mukutan and Galdessa, both of which rank among the most spectacular travel experiences we've ever had.

When describing a place as refined as Kuki Gallmann's Mukutan Retreat at Ol Ari Nyiro ranch in Laikipia, it's somehow crude to begin with the food. But, *man.* Mukutan's resident cook, Simon, has worked for Gallmann nearly since the day she moved to Kenya from Italy twenty years ago. In that time he has perfected a form of culinary fusion that's part traditional Italian, part

Galdessa decor is part Out of Africa, *part "Flintstones."*

whatever's growing in the garden or swimming in the ponds that dot Gallmann's 100,000-acre property. Upon our arrival, Simon's opening salvo—scooped avocado with boiled crayfish salad, julienne carrots, and mango ice cream for dessert—had us slapping high fives at the table like football fans.

So the food is very good at Mukutan. But then so is everything else that reflects Gallmann's elegant touch. Gallmann designed three guest *bandas* (quarters) on the site to be simultaneously private and wall-less, maximizing the dramatic view of Mukutan Gorge at the property's feet. From every perch in our banda—the canopy bed, the bath, the writing desk, the toilet—we could see baboons, buffalo, et al. snacking at an adjacent salt lick.

Mukutan's guests are encouraged to explore Ol Ari Nyiro at their own pace, especially the thermal spring that's been corralled into a magical outdoor hot tub within shower-shoe shambling distance of the bandas. A resident host is on call to chaperone visitors on more ambitious hikes through the bush in search of buffalo, black rhino, and whatever other creatures they're able to glimpse through the shoulder-height brambles. It's hard trekking, perfect for restimulating an appetite after one of Simon's staggering meals.

A stay at Mukutan costs $800 per night all inclusive. Call it a once-in-a-lifetime experience, and don't let the price tag get in the way of enjoying every moment. For more information, contact Mukutan at 011-254-2-521220 or Park East Tours at 800-223-6078.

Galdessa, in the heart of Tszavo East National Park (two-thirds of the way from Nairobi to the Kenyan coast), is astonishing long before you spot your first elephant. Dozens of ingenious little details indoors catch your eye first: bedside lamp shades fashioned from ostrich eggs; water pitchers sheathed in brilliant Masai beads on the room-service tray; vertebrae embedded in the bathroom plaster that serve as towel pegs or candleholders, depending on your mood. The level of luxury they aim for here would be ambitious in midtown Manhattan. Deep in the heart of the African bush, it's baffling.

After the initial shock of your arrival wears off, the physical beauty of the landscape begins to register. Galdessa fronts on the Galana River, a narrow band of green vegetation in an otherwise dry landscape. On the opposite shore from camp is the Yatta Plateau, a flat expanse of hardened lava that seemingly stretches all the way to prehistory.

When the animals show up, a primal sort of sensory overload kicks in, and everything begins to make absurdly perfect sense. Huge, reddish (from the soil) elephants tramping silently through the bush mere feet from your Land Rover? Sure. Vervet monkeys prancing from limb to limb in a tree overhanging your dining table? Of course. Vicious-looking crocodiles and comically uncomfortable hippos wallowing in the river? Let's stop for some fishing.

A note for honeymooners: Galdessa's youthful staff enjoys a good prank above all else, and they're not above serving the occasional elephant-dung cake to unsuspecting couples. If you cannot puncture your dessert beyond the icing (and if everyone else in the dining room is clutching their stomachs with laughter), you've been had.

We stayed in the honeymoon suite, distinguished from Galdessa's other bandas by its oversized bed, distance to the main lodge, and a soaking tub at the foot of the sitting porch. If it's available, grab it—but all the facilities are similarly marvelous.

For more information, call 011-254-2-890635, E-mail geneva@galdessa.com, or visit www.galdessa.com. Or call Park East Tours at 800-223-6078.

Elsewhere in Africa

Eloping in Africa is limited by the unwillingness of many local wedding consultants to deal with short notice and several African nations' Byzantine marriage laws. There are some exceptions:

Masai Mara

When in the Masai Mara, do as the Masai do. The bride and groom are dressed separately near the wedding site in full Masai attire: red robes and beads for the woman, a spear for the man. A Masai religious elder conducts the ceremony, after which the villagers in attendance have been known to break into their distinctive jumping dance. For more information, contact Lonrho Hotels at 800-845-3692.

Zimbabwe

Tongabezi Lodge on Livingston Island is mere minutes from one of the world's great natural wonders, Victoria Falls. Guests stay in luxurious tents and feast on gourmet meals, accompanied by the sound of splashing hippos in the Zambezi River and, of course, the falls. Tongabezi wedding options abound: couples may be married at a vista overlooking the majestic falls, on the backs of elephants. They can even incorporate bungee jumps from the Victoria Falls Bridge. For more information, call Classic Encounters at 212-972-0031, or E-mail gowildsa@aol.com.

Masai weddings are colorful affairs, to say the least.
(Jean Walden)

Namibia

The Sossusvlei Dunes in Namibia, southwest Africa, rise one thousand feet above a surrounding plain—a spectacle that attracts photographers from all over the world. Hot-air balloons are ideal for soaking in the spectacle and for staging an airborne wedding ceremony. For more information, contact Classic Encounters at 212-972-0031, or E-mail gowildsa@aol.com.

South Africa

South Africa is a huge place, with myriad eloping options. Couples can exchange vows in a hot-air balloon above a game park or in wine country, during a journey from Pretoria to Cape Town on a luxury train, or on a beach amid thousands of penguins.

At *Tongabezi Lodge* on Livingston Island, guests can stay in a genuine *treehouse.* (Courtesy of Tongabezi Lodge)

At the village of Lesedi, just north of Johannesburg, families from the Zulu warrior nation, Xhosa, Pedi, and the Basotho live in traditional-style homesteads. Guests are encouraged to learn their cultures and traditions and to integrate these elements into their ceremonies. For more information, call Classic Encounters at 212-972-0031, or E-mail gowildsa@aol.com.

Nuts and Bolts

Where to Start

Lonrho Hotels' itemized wedding services include help with the procurement of a marriage license ($268) and marriage officer ($266), and extras such as Chuka drummers ($280) and a choir ($496) for the ceremony, dinner ($40 per person), camel transportation, flowers, and so on. For more information, contact Lonrho Hotels at 800-845-3692.

Travel Information

Most major European airlines service Jomo Kenyatta International Airport in Nairobi. We flew Northwest Airlines overnight from San Francisco to Minneapolis to Amsterdam, and KLM overnight from Amsterdam to Nairobi. For more information, contact Northwest at 800-225-2525 and KLM at 800-374-7747.

Most Mount Kenya Safari Club guests usually travel from Nairobi to the club via safari bus, per prior arrangement with a tour company. Manhattan-based Park East Tours handled all the logistics for our safari except the wedding itself, and there wasn't a single misstep the entire time. Before our departure, Park East helped us procure our visas and supplied us with a goodies bag that included a journal, a detailed itinerary, and a very handy list of frequently asked questions about Africa, which we referred to often. The brochure-sized pamphlet begins "Jambo. You have just learned how to say 'hello' all across East Africa." So true.

Park East Tours representatives met us at the airport in Nairobi, drove us in comfortable vans from lodge to lodge, and even supplied a cooler of bottled water for us to drink en route. For more information, call Park East Tours' New York office at 800-223-6078 or 212-765-4870, or see www.parkeast.com.

Legal Requirements

To obtain a marriage license in Kenya you'll need your passports, two copies of the first three pages of both passports, and two copies of your birth certificates. Divorcees must have certified divorce papers (two copies, in English). Those who are widowed must have their late spouse's death certificate (two copies, in English).

Typically, marriage licenses in Kenya require two weeks to obtain. But fast-track licenses are available at the attorney general's office in Nairobi—at a price. *Do not try any of this on your own.* Lonrho Hotels supplies wedding couples with a chaperone. Ours, Joseph, proved to be beyond essential in navigating the Attorney General Building's mazelike hallways and securing the attention of indifferent civil servants. We spent a full day pursuing our marriage license, a process that was not fun but did allow us to break through the bubble of isolation that typically surrounds tourists and see everyday Kenyan life up close.

It may help your cause if you dress up a bit for the attorney general's office, meaning leave the shorts and T-shirts in the backpack that day.

Lead Time

United States citizens are required to obtain visas through the Kenyan consulate before they enter the country. Your safari operator will be able to help push this through.

Immunizations are another obstacle to eloping in Kenya on a whim. You'll want to protect yourself against hepatitis, malaria, yellow fever, typhoid, polio, and tetanus. Your local international travel clinic will advise you on what specific shots and vaccines you need and how far in advance of your departure you need to begin taking them. Generally speaking, you'll want to get started at least a month ahead of your date of departure.

You'll need to arrive in Nairobi a minimum of three days in advance of your ceremony to procure the marriage license at the attorney general's office. Three days is about all Lonrho Hotels needs to assemble the parts of your ceremony as well.

When to Go

The central highlands, where the Mount Kenya Safari Club is located, enjoy the best weather in all of Kenya. It's essentially springlike year-round, although April through June and September through December are relatively rainy. During these months there are fewer animals to see (they're dispersed over a wider range of territory) but also fewer tourists to contend with.

Additional Contact Information

For general information about travel in Kenya, contact the Kenya Consulate and Tourism Office at 212-486-1300.

Recommended Reading

Some obvious choices are *Out of Africa* by Isak Dinesen (Karen Blixen), *The Flame Trees of Thika* by Elspeth Huxley, and just about anything Africa oriented by Ernest Hemingway. *The Snows of Kilimanjaro* is a personal favorite. Also, if you come across a copy of *The Weather in Africa* by Martha Gellhorn (Hemingway's ex), grab it. She's rarely read, but great. Kuki Gallmann's account of her life at Ol Ari Nyiro ranch in Laikipia, *I Dreamed of Africa*, is essential reading if you're planning to visit Mukutan. A Hollywood movie based on the memoir is in the pipeline.

Borneo

Cost: $$$

Degree of difficulty: Doable

Borneo is one of those places whose mention starts the imagination spinning. Impenetrable jungles thick with hardwoods. Insects the size of a human hand. Indigenous people clinging to a way of life so old that modern sensibilities find it utterly fascinating and strange. Borneo is the island keeper of all things exotic, and to some people exotic and romantic are one and the same.

Ken Knezick, the gregarious president of Texas-based Island Dreams, a travel company specializing in dive trips to Asian islands, is one of those people. When Knezick decided to marry, no simple walk down the aisle would do. Instead he imagined a ceremony infused with decidedly un-Western traditions, a fabulous Malaysian feast, a honeymoon house built on stilts, and a week of spectacular diving in the Sulawesi Sea. Though the Malaysian authorities said it couldn't be done, Knezick persisted and eventually pulled off the wedding he had in mind. Island Dreams now duplicates the experience for similarly unconventional souls.

Island Dreams Borneo weddings begin with a civil ceremony in Kota Kinabalu, the capital of Sabah, Borneo. The setting is your basic low-light registry office. But it's not lifeless; the space usually is filled with a vibrant mix of Chinese businessmen, sons and

Orangutans are indigenous to Borneo, but the best way to see them is in one of the country's several orangutan rehabilitation centers.

daughters of tattooed headhunters, Indians, and Malays. From the registry office, couples are escorted to the city's cultural center via a Toyota Land Cruiser covered in orchids and birds of paradise. Here's where things get ethnic in earnest.

The cultural center in Kinabalu is a kind of living museum, and a traditional Kadazan longhouse is built right on the grounds. The majority of Sabah's indigenous peoples are Kadazan, and whole communities live in single longhouses built on stilts so as to guard against floods and (in a not-so-distant past) warring tribes. Each longhouse has a central hallway with as many as twenty rooms off to the side. Families live one to a room, but the day's activities—weaving, carving, haircutting, dancing, and drinking rice wine—take place in the hallway. Every family has its own stash of homemade rice wine.

For their ceremony at the cultural center, couples can elect to wear traditional Kadazan wedding attire: full-length, jet black velvety sarongs (metric measurements should be faxed beforehand). The groom is topped with a turban. The bride's costume is covered with elaborate gold braid. Before entering the longhouse, participants remove their shoes and blessed water is sprinkled at the doorway. The bride and groom then enter the house beneath a conical hat meant to keep any ill spirits from joining the festivities. Though the officiant is hard to understand without the aid of a translator, one thing that's perfectly clear is the admonition that the groom have one wife. Apparently, some wealthy Malays have taken to marrying several.

The reception dinner is a feast best eaten with the fingers. Guests sit on grass mats while the food, which typically includes grilled fish, chicken, and beef spiced with ginger and peppers, is served on long, low tables. Rice wine, fermented in earthen jugs buried underground, is consumed liberally. Malay wedding cake is a kind of glutinous sweet rice wrapped in banana leaves, though a six-tiered Western wedding cake (covered in fresh rose petals) is available.

There are only two consequences to watch out for following a Kadazan wedding: a rice wine hangover, and sore facial muscles from smiling so much.

Kota Kinabalu is a major city and, with the exception of the cultural center, not particularly exotic. After the ceremony, Knezick can arrange for a short flight to the city of Tawau and a drive to the village of Semporna. There rests the Dragon Inn, a guest house whose octagonal cabanas are built on stilts. The Dragon Inn isn't luxurious; a bamboo-and-woodsy smell hangs in the air and the rooms are sparsely furnished. But it definitely is exotic. Knezick ranks it among his favorite places to stay in the world.

Tanjung Puting National Park

The sight of orangutans in the wild has been known to make grown men cry. Maybe it's the innocence in their quarter-sized eyes. Or the way orang mothers care for their young. Probably it has something to do with the primates' undeniable likeness to humanity. Whatever the reason, orangutans melt hearts.

Tanjung Puting National Park, located near the town of Pangkalanbun, acts as both a sanctuary for wild orangutans and a rehabilitation center where orangutans are reintroduced into their natural habitat after a time in captivity. At feeding times, what at first appears as an uninhabited jungle canopy fills with the shaking and rustling of orangs in pursuit of bananas. Many orangutans are Homo sapiens savvy and will climb right into visitors' laps.

There are two good lodging options for couples who want to visit Pangkalanbun. The most upscale local digs are found at Rimba Lodge, located inside the park. Rooms are casual but have some flair; guests sleep on Indonesian batik sheets and a mosquito net drapes nearly to the floor. The other choice is to hire a private *klotok* (motorized longboat) for two or three days. Each boat comes with a cook and a captain, and accesses the least-visited areas of the park. At night the boat docks in isolated jungle coves in which gibbons and proboscis monkeys frolic. A proboscis monkey's nose looks something like a half-full water balloon.

Rimba Lodge is rarely booked, but occasionally a tour group will fill the place up. Reservations can be made through Hotel Blue in Pangkalanbun at 011-62-532-

21211. To hire a boat, write to: Jl. Idris Rt. 6 No 507, Kumai Hulu 74181 Pangkalanbun, Kalimantan Tengah.

Underwater Weddings

Where you find scuba fans, you find underwater weddings—except in Fiji, for some reason. Oh well. There are plenty of others to choose from here.

Sipadan Island Dive Resort arranges underwater weddings in Malaysian Borneo. Sipadan is home to some of the most exotic coral in the world and has been featured in *National Geographic*. Underwater weddings here are slightly different than most: the divers are equipped with underwater communication devices that link them to a minister, who officiates from the pier. For more information, contact Kenneth Knezick at Island Dreams (800-346-6116) or E-mail Ken@islandream.com.

Atlantis Dive Center in Key Largo capitalizes on Florida's elopement-friendly marriage laws (see Florida chapter in Part III), and a fantastic wedding site: an underwater statue known as the Christ of the Abyss twenty-five minutes from the dock. For more information, contact Atlantis Dive Center at 800-331-DIVE (800-331-3483) or E-mail atlantis@pennekamp.com.

Tradewinds Charters organizes underwater weddings in Hawaii's breathtaking Hanauma Bay, a thriving marine preserve (see Hawaii chapter in Part III). Tradewinds provides a scuba-proficient minister, and a professional underwater wedding photographer and videographer to boot. For more information, call 808-973-0311 or E-mail captken@pixi.com.

Nuts and Bolts

Where to Start

Texas-based Island Dreams is the place to call for a traditional Kadazan wedding. Expect to pay around $2,000, depending on the details—ceremonies can be completely tailor-made. For more information, call 800-346-6116.

Travel Information

Island Dreams will arrange to get you to Malaysia, usually on Malaysian Air Lines. The flight from Los Angeles takes a full day. Interisland boat transport also is arranged.

Legal Requirements

Mostly because of the good relationship between Ken Knezick and the local government in Kota Kinabalu, the legal process is surprisingly easy. Though foreign weddings in Malaysia are still rare, most of the legal requirements can be taken care of prior to departure. It may take a fax or two, but in any case, all you need to bring is a passport.

Lead Time

You'll need to give Island Dreams about a week to pull together a Kadazan wedding. If you plan to visit the rain forest while you're in Borneo, which you'd be crazy not to do, you'll need to get the appropriate inoculations. This requires a few weeks' advance planning.

When to Go

Monsoon season is in January and February—don't elope in Borneo then. The eight months between April and November have the most consistently beautiful weather.

Mexico

Cost: $$

Degree of difficulty: Doable

The southernmost tip of Baja California is where the cold Pacific, pounding in from the west, tangles with the warmer, gentler Sea of Cortez. Some say the exact point where the two bodies connect is a tiny cove in Cabo San Lucas where the water streams in from both sides and is sheltered from the tumult of the open sea. The symbolism of such a union was not lost on the person who named the cove Playa del Amante (Lover's Beach).

It's hard to imagine that nature could create a more perfect wedding spot. Since it is only accessible by boat, Lover's Beach is one of the more secluded Cabo coves. Rugged desert shrubs and steep cliffs make it unreachable and unviewable from the road—most visitors don't even know it exists. Sunset shades the sand and wind-carved rock in multiple hues and lights the water seemingly from all directions.

Traci and Richard Abbott were married in Cabo San Lucas in 1997. Since they made the arrangements themselves, they decided against the boat-access-only wedding spot; at the time, they thought it would be too complicated. Instead, they married at a restaurant overlooking the beach. It was beautiful, they say, but not ideal. What's more, during the rest of their stay, the Abbotts often found themselves fumbling for directions in their

Cabo San Lucas, where the cold Pacific tangles with the Sea of Cortez
(The Mexico Ministry of Tourism)

rental car or scrambling for information about local marriage customs—details they wished they had been told ahead of time. The experience inspired the couple to create a company, Land's End Weddings, that helps fellow romantics learn from their mistakes. The Abbotts are now experts at arranging ceremonies at various locations throughout Cabo, including Lover's Beach.

From their home in Canada, the Abbotts work with Cabo-based partner Cecilia Torres to take care of all the particulars. Couples are picked up at their hotel and driven to fill out the necessary paperwork in town. The day of their Lover's Beach wedding, Land's End hires a water taxi to take them from town to the cove, where flowers and an officiant await, along with a solo guitarist. (You can even hire a full mariachi band if you wish. But remember, it's a small cove.)

Couples write their own vows, which can be timed to coincide with the setting sun. The water taxi returns at a prearranged time, and the boat ride back to the marina is quick, peaceful, and just cool enough for cuddling.

Elsewhere in Mexico

Pacific Coves

It's no secret that, during certain times of the year, Cabo's main beaches are packed with tourists fighting for towel space on the sand. But when the water is calm, Playa Bahia Chileno (Chilean Beach) just up the coast provides a perfect launch spot for kayaks, which are available for rent mere steps from the water. From Chilean Beach, it's possible to paddle up the coast for hours, accessing dozens of romantic bays, semisecluded beaches, and crowd-free snorkeling. To get to Chilean Beach from Cabo San Lucas, drive up the highway to Km. 15 and look for the dive flag on the side of the road.

Santa Maria Beach has a little bay with its own blue lagoon. Just offshore is a coral reef that has been spared the abuses of some of the more popular snorkel spots. Nearby Twin Dolphin Beach is another quiet landing spot with foot access to some unnamed coves a little farther west that are even quieter still. From there, paddle a half-mile more to Playa Barco Varado (Shipwreck Beach), named for the Japanese freighter wreckage that sits on the sand. For a guided trip, drive east on Highway 1 to San José del Cabo, where two operators (Nomadas del Baja and Los Lobos del Mar) located on the main beach offer half- or full-day excursions to the coves.

Tres Fuentes Inn

The Tres Fuentes Inn is a secluded bed-and-breakfast that was purchased by its American owners, Mark and Kimberley Lemyre, just after their own Cabo honeymoon several years ago. The Lemyres renovated the old Mexico–style villa so that each of the eight rooms is decorated to represent a different Baja city. The Cabo San Lucas room is adorned (tactfully) with pirate paraphernalia to commemorate the swashbucklers who used to plunder from its coves in the late 1500s.

Though it's just a five-minute walk from Cabo's main strip, the Tres Fuentes Inn is sheltered from the din of nearby clubs and resorts—all you'll hear in your room is a steady trickle from three courtyard fountains. Breakfasts, which include a traditional hot Mexican entrée, are served outdoors. For more information, see www.mexonline.com/fountain.htm, contact the inn via E-mail (3fuentes@cabonet.net.mx), or phone 800-711-5189 or 011-52-114-3-52-00.

Nuts and Bolts

Where to Start

Land's End Weddings' basic package comprises the services of a judge and help with the arrangements, including a blood test. It costs $800. Location fees are an additional $50 to $100. Lover's Beach is at the higher end of the spectrum due to the cost of transporting the bride, groom, and entourage. Photography, a videographer, music, and flowers also are available at additional, itemized expense.

Though the Abbotts run Land's End Weddings from their home in British Columbia, contacts in Cabo take care of the

details. For more information, call 604-485-4889 or see www
.prcn.org/wedding/.

Travel Information

Los Cabos International Airport is serviced by Alaska Airlines,
Mexicana, Aero Mexico, Aero California, America West,
Continental, and American Airlines. Shuttle service to Cabo San
Lucas from the airport costs approximately $20.

Legal Requirements

Upon arrival, Land's End Weddings helps you take care of the particulars, including the requisite blood test. You will need to bring
your birth certificates, tourist cards (which are handed out on the
plane), and passports or driver's licenses. Divorcees need legal
proof that they have been separated for more than a year. Land's
End Weddings provides four required witnesses for a nominal fee.
It is important to know that each region in Mexico has its own
marriage/elopement laws for foreigners. Cabo San Lucas's are
quite good, but if you are planning to wed somewhere else in
Mexico, you need to check the laws for that region.

Lead Time

Mexican law requires that you be in the country at least three days
before getting married. Land's End Weddings does not need much
more advance notice than that, but they appreciate as much time
as you can give them.

When to Go

Cabo is at its most crowded (read, least romantic) during heavy
tourist times: Christmas, New Year's, spring break, and Semana
Santa (the week before Easter). If you manage to avoid the crowds,

the only remaining obstacle is the rainy season, which peaks in the summertime. That leaves fall and mid-to-late spring as the wedding seasons of choice. Of course, there's a reason Cabo is so crowded during the winter—that's when the weather is at its most predictably excellent.

Additional Contact Information

Mexican Government Tourism offices all over the United States will be more than happy to inundate you with brochures and can be reached at 213-351-2069. A useful website is www.loscabos guide.com.

Appendix

As we noted in the introduction, *Beyond Vegas* is not intended to be used as a travel guidebook. To write a true guidebook about a place, you must immerse yourself in the local life in a way that a brief visit for the purposes of getting married does not allow.

We do, however, know a thing or two about eloping. Over the course of the year we spent researching this book we eloped ten times. Along the way we picked up a few nuggets of wisdom that cut across boundaries and are as true in Kenya as in Nevada. This appendix is a repository for our gold.

Items to Take with You

Your Own Camera, Film, and Lead-Lined Bag

If your logistics don't include the services of a professional photographer, someone inevitably will volunteer to help take snapshots. But this largesse can be a double-edged sword: you hand your camera to a hotel porter, you take your chances in the expertise department. One way to exert at least a smidgen of control over the situation is to bring your own camera and film. That way you can be sure the equipment works, even if a few heads and feet may be cut off in the bargain. Though airport x-ray machines purportedly are film-safe, a lead-lined film bag provides considerable peace of mind.

Travel Steamer

This little plastic contraption will run you $30 or so at the travel store, but will prove invaluable if a wrinkle-free wedding dress is a priority item. A corollary to this would be a quality hanging bag—save money elsewhere in your arsenal of luggage.

Makeup

Brides, you'll want to look pretty out there, no matter where you're headed. And foreign makeup can get a little odd in both color and consistency.

Bubble Bath, Candles, and Incense

It is your wedding night, after all. Better not leave the nuances to chance or the gift shop buyer's tastes.

Pepto Bismol Chewables

Prewedding jitters combined with airline and foreign food can be hard on the stomach. These pink little pills are equal parts portable and effective.

A Poster Tube

You'll need this for transporting your marriage license (a treasured souvenir, as well as necessary proof of your wedding) home worry free.

Love Means Never Having to Ask What to Tip

What to tip the people who help your elopement come off is no small issue. It's our experience that, even with package deals in which all costs have been arranged beforehand, it's still entirely appropriate

to slip the officiant a little something extra to express your gratitude—especially when you're talking about religious ceremonies.

The thing is, determining the appropriate amount to tip can
be, in the words of Winston Churchill, a riddle shrouded in mys-
tery. When we solicited Rabbi Boyden in Israel to tell us the appropriate amount of shekels with which we could express our
appreciation for his flexibility and spirit of adventure, the man
turned three shades of green. Ditto Pastor Pearson in Nevada and
Reverend Montgomery in Scotland. Even the person translating
for the Hindu celebrant in Bali was reluctant to say the number
out loud.

So here's what we did. The equivalent of U.S.$200 is the ceil-
ing around the world—a tip that will be considered generous but
not blow up the curve. Adjust backward from that in $25 incre-
ments for the amount of lead time given, time spent at the ceremony, personableness, and general artistic impression.

Finding Information

Preliminary Phone Calls

There's a world of eloping options out there beyond what's
depicted in *Beyond Vegas*. In Maui alone, there must be a dozen
or more tour companies and wedding coordinators offering their
services. We chose to highlight one that caught our eye. If we have
piqued your interest, and you have the seed of an idea that's not
here, we recommend you do what we did: pick up the phone.

Tourism Boards

Tourism boards are often, but not always, hooked into a network
of local wedding professionals. And those names that are handed
over tend to be tried, trusted, and true. A good place to start.

Tour Operators

Tour operators specialize in the destination you have in mind, often know people in the local wedding industry, or have been looking for an excuse to pull together a wedding themselves. If you're willing to be human guinea pigs, you may even get a break on the price in exchange for the experience!

A good source for locating tour operators all over the world is Specialty Travel Index, a private company that publishes a quarterly magazine and now has a spiffy website (www.specialty travel.com). It is a glorified yellow pages for specialty travel tour operators around the globe that's been in business for a while and generally only lists reputable operators.

The Concierge Desk

If you can identify a reputable hotel in the vicinity of where you're intending to go, the concierge probably has at least been asked about weddings—and likely has pulled off more than a few.

The Knot

This hip and happening website (and burgeoning publishing company) has, among other eloping resources, past issues of *Honeymoon Magazine* on-line. They have a wealth of information about destination weddings, which aren't exactly the same thing as eloping but will get you in the ballpark. Visit the site at www.theknot.com.

Expect to experience at least a modicum of resistance if you try and convince a destination wedding planner to handle your elopement. This industry, like the conventional wedding professionals in your own neighborhood, much prefer lavish affairs with longer lead times—and higher commissions. But it's definitely worth a shot, especially during dead spots in the travel season.

Consulates

Consulates surely are up to speed on wedding laws, visas, and the like. They're less likely to know or recommend specific tour operators or wedding planners. Certainly worth a call.

If your local metropolis lacks a consulate, New York is a sure bet as a backup. Phone numbers for a few New York consulates:

Australia: 212-351-6500

Canada: 212-596-1783

Costa Rica: 212-509-3066

Greece: 212-988-5800

Israel: 212-499-5000

Italy: 212-737-9100

Switzerland: 212-599-4230

United Kingdom: 212-745-0277

Contact Information for Airlines

Air Canada: 800-776-3000

Air Jamaica: 888-452-6247

Air Pacific: 800-227-4446

Alitalia: 800-223-5730

American Airlines: 800-223-5436

British Airways: 800-247-9297

Continental: 800-525-0280

Delta: 800-221-1212 (domestic); 800-241-1414
   (international)

El Al Airlines: 800-223-6700

Hawaiian Airlines: 800-367-5320

KLM: 800-374-7747

Lufthansa: 800-645-3880

Malaysia Airlines: 800-552-9264

Mexicana: 800-531-7921

Northwest Airlines: 800-225-2525
Olympic Airways: 800-223-1226
Saeta: 305-341-8913
Swissair: 800-221-4750
Tower Air: 800-221-2500
United Airlines: 800-241-6522
US Airways: 800-428-4322
Virgin Atlantic Airways: 800-862-8621

Some Final Words of Advice

Try and *avoid eloping during holidays* or the high tourist season wherever you want to go. In addition to wreaking havoc with lead times, tourist pressure can set hotel concierges and local wedding coordinators on edge, and these are the people you'll want to set the tone. Saturdays are by far the most popular with brides the world around. Weekdays, during the day, everyone's availability skyrockets.

Always mention you're on your honeymoon when you check into your hotel. Between the time you board the elevator with your bags and the moment you slip your key in the door, more often than not management will have placed a bottle of champagne in an ice bucket beside the bed—or upgraded you altogether.

Never let anyone tell you it can't be done.

Index